DONALD TRUMP'S SECOND COMING: Is Democracy Dead, Dying or Alive,

An Anthology of Literature and Art from Africa and North America, Volume 4

Curated and Edited by:
Tendai Rinos Mwanaka

Mwanaka Media and Publishing Pvt Ltd,
Chitungwiza Zimbabwe
*
Creativity, Wisdom and Beauty

Publisher: *Mmap*
Mwanaka Media and Publishing Pvt Ltd
24 Svosve Road, Zengeza 1
Chitungwiza Zimbabwe
mwanaka@yahoo.com
mwanaka13@gmail.com
www.africanbookscollective.com/publishers/mwanaka-media-and-publishing
https://facebook.com/MwanakaMediaAndPublishing/

Distributed in and outside N. America by African Books Collective
orders@africanbookscollective.com
www.africanbookscollective.com

ISBN: 978-1-77928-211-8
EAN: 9781779282118

© Tendai Rinos Mwanaka 2025

All rights reserved.
No part of this book may be reproduced or transmitted in any form or by any means, mechanical or electronic, including photocopying and recording, or be stored in any information storage or retrieval system, without written permission from the publisher

DISCLAIMER
All views expressed in this publication are those of the author and do not necessarily reflect the views of *Mmap*.

About Editor

Tendai Rinos Mwanaka is a multidisciplinary artist, editor, publisher and producer with over 70 individual books and curated anthologies published in US, Northern Ireland, UK, Cameroon and Zimbabwe. He has 5 music albums, with a new album, *For Mberikwazvo: The Winter After* (2025) recently released. His music is playing in at least 18 radio stations in US, Canada, UK, France, Israel, Brazil and Australia. He has hundreds of paintings and drawings, thousands of photographs, some exhibited, some published and some sold. His pieces have appeared in over 500 journals in over 35 countries and his books and writing are translated into at least 11 languages. His music can be licensed here: https://www.songtradr.com/tendai.mwanaka. Find him here: https://m.facebook.com/tendai.mwanaka

Table of Contents

Eshu's Post-Dated Poem: C. Liegh McInnis
A Poem For Palestine: *Tendai Rinos Mwanaka*
Fill in the dots: of Holocaust Enablers: *Tendai Rinos Mwanaka*
I am so scared, Please help me!: *Tendai Rinos Mwanaka*
Poo-spewing Rudy with a Mussolini Flag: *Bob McNeil*
Migrants: *Paris J Smith*
Sympathy for Uncle Sam: *Bob McNeil*
The battlefield of poverty: *Abigail George*
Yesterday: *Abigail George*
When I have a problem with myself, I write really bad poetry: *Abigail George*
Donald Trump has been president for a month now: *Charlie R. Braxton*
The Red Wave of Enslavement: *Bob McNeil*
Letter from the future: *Edgar Manuel Cambaza*
Abe Abiding: *JB Pravda*
I have another dream: *Edgar Manuel Cambaza*
The woke shall be awaken: *Edgar Manuel Cambaza*
The Mythological People of Color Coalition: *C Liegh McInnis*
The Terror Called Trump: *Bob McNeil*
Look at Us: *Isaac Kilibwa*
Healing: *Isaac Kilibwa*
Healing: *Isaac Kilibwa*
Ruins: *Isaac Kilibwa*

ManSwanSong: *JB Pravda*
A Bell for Danny Martin: *Tim Hall*
To the Unknown Proletarian: *Tim Hall*
"From Diplomacy to Innovation: The Changing Landscape of U.S.-Africa Relations": *Onward Mutapurwa*
Trump humping Sam: *Bob McNeil*
Curated Selections from myactivity.google.com: *Tiffany L. Hendrix*
From ramblings of A House Wife: *Bahiirwa Catherine*
Shadows of Democracy: *Mthokozisi Ncube*
The Trump Effect: *Mthokozisi Ncube*
Beyond the Phenomenon: *Mthokozisi Ncube*
"This or That?": Voting for Vice President Kamala Harris Despite Democratic Debacle and Cowardice: *C Liegh McInnis*
Grass: *Cheryl Caesar*
The occupied: *Cheryl Caesar*
Aftermath: *Cheryl Caesar*
Portrait of Frances Perkins: *Cheryl Ceaser*
It must be...: *William Khalipwina Mpina*
And gods have never slept: *William Khalipwina Mpina*
Show me, don't tell me...; *William Khalipwina Mpina*
How Trump Tried To Bully African Countries With Used Clothes: *Charlie R. Braxton*
LIBERTY'S LAMENT TO THE GILDED TYRANT: *Emman Usman Shehu*
THE NEW AGENT ORANGE: *Emman Usman Shehu*

She Loves You, Yeah, Yeah.....And You Know That Can't Be Bad: Al E.'s Equation Was Too Square, Hers Rocks– 'L(ove) T(aken)=L(uv) M(ade): Joseph B Pravda

EinstiniusGermanicusRoaminNumeralDuo: *Joseph B. Pravda*

Pesti/Geno-cide: *Gerard Sarnat*

tanka (Trump 2.0's Riviera): *Gerard Sarnat*

BLITZKREIG 2.0: *Gerard Sarnat*

Donald Trump au prisme de la science de Claude Bernard : entre crise démocratique et renaissance: *Luc Koffi*

Contributors' Bio Notes

Bahiirwa Catherine is a twenty eight year old female Ugandan who is a literature enthusiast who graduated with honors with a literature major from Makerere University in Uganda. A few of her works have been published in the Best New African Poets anthology of 2021 and the Uganda at 60 poetry collection.

C. Liegh McInnis is a poet, short story writer, Prince scholar, 2025 Finalist for the Mississippi Poet Laureate, co-founder of the Jackson State Creative Writing Program, former editor/publisher of *Black Magnolias*, and author of eight books—four collections of poetry, one collection of short fiction (*Scripts: Sketches and Tales of Urban Mississippi*), one work of literary criticism (*The Lyrics of Prince: A Literary Look*), one co-authored work, *Brother Hollis: The Sankofa of a Movement Man*, discussing Mississippi Civil Rights icon, and former First Runner-Up of the Amiri Baraka/Sonia Sanchez Poetry Award. Additionally, he has been published in periodicals and anthologies.

Cheryl Caesar is a writer, teacher of writing and visual artist living in Lansing. She is an associate professor at Michigan State University, and does research and advocacy for culturally-responsive pedagogy. She has written a chapbook of anti-Trump poems, *Flatman (Thurston Howl Publications)*. Her poetry has appeared in publications in Australia, Bangladesh, Canada, India, Singapore, the United Kingdom, the United States, Yemen and Zimbabwe.

Charlie R. Braxton is a poet, playwright, and cultural critic who writes about music and politics. He is the author of three volumes of verse, *Ascension From The Ashes (Blackwood Press,1990), Cinders Rekindled (Jawara Press, 2012), and Embers Among The Ashes: Poems In A Haiku Manner (Jawara Press, 2018)*. His latest volume of verse is entitled *And The Earth Cried Blood* will be available in February on Jawara Press at lulu.com

Tiffany L. Hendrix teaches five classes in two languages in a public high school in Colorado, U.S., for now. She was a history major. It's a hard time to be a history major. Her poems have recently been published in *Vine Leaves Press* and *Creative Guts*. Find her @originalgeotrix on social media.

Edgar Manuel Cambaza (sometimes under the pen name Jorge d'Amizad) is a Mozambican writer, poet, and author of the literary works *Gaia, Seven Seconds, and O Menino de Bié [The Boy of Bié]*. His poetry and short stories explore themes of identity, nature, and human emotion and have been featured internationally, including in *Experimental Writing: Africa vs. Latin America and Nationalism: (Mis)Understanding Donald Trump's Capitalism, Racism, Global Politics, International Trade, and Media Wars*. Alongside his creative writing, he maintains an active academic career with public health, ethics, and science publications.

Onward Mutapurwa is a Zimbabwean citizen and a graduate in Politics and Public Management from Midlands State University. A passionate advocate for climate change and digital inclusion, he has contributed to several anthologies, including the *Best New African Poets and Zimbolicious*. Currently, he collaborates on a mental health awareness anthology and an article exploring SADC and sustainable development goals. As an editorial intern at The Social Talks, Onward has written on topics such as Biden's U.S. elections and the DRC as a geopolitical chessboard. His articles on Chinese diplomacy and research philosophy are featured on *Academia.edu*.

Mthokozisi Ncube, who hails from the village of Mlomwe, Plumtree and affectionately known as Imbongi Yabantu is a renowned multilingual writer, poet and the founder of AbaseMaNcubeni Writers' Associate (AWA) – a non-profit making organisation enhanced to help in preserving the African Languages and its culture; through uplifting and helping the up-and-coming writers in publishing their unpublished works, especially those who find it difficult to access publishing houses. He is an award winner both local and international with five solo published books including *'Kwakusempini', 'Lakanye Wangenza', 'Still I Hope', 'Zidla Belindile'* and *'When Darkness Engulfs'*.

William Khalipwina Mpina is a distinguished literary Malawian figure renowned for his contributions to poetry and literature. He co-edited *Walking the Battlefield (2020)*, a bilingual anthology of poems reflecting on the Covid-19 pandemic, and authored *Mooning the Morning (2022)*, published by Montfort Media. Also, he wrote *Kamwala Kodabwitsa (2024)* as part of the Invisible Child Project, funded by Pen International. His most recent work is a short story collection, *Stranger in Her Own Skin (2025)*, published by *Mwanaka Media and Publishing*. Mpina holds significant roles as Treasurer General of the Malawi Union of Academic and Nonfiction Authors and as an Executive Committee member of Pen Malawi, a local chapter of Pen International.

Late-phase often graphic poet arrived in seventh decade, aphorist, humorist or sometimes meanderist; **Gerard Sarnat's** a multiple Pushcart/Best of Net Award nominee. Activism Through Poetry: How Gerard Sarnat Uses Verse as a Form of Protest is a 2025 retrospective: https://culterateblog.wordpress.com/2025/02/20/activism-through-poetry-how-gerard-sarnat-uses-verse-as-a-form-of-protest/. His work's been widely published; including four collections; *by Rattle, London Arts-Based Research Centre, Israel Association of Writers in English, The Nature of Our Times/Poets For Science, Gravity of the Thing, Brooklyn Review, Tokyo Poetry Journal, Gargoyle, New Delta Review, Buddhist Review, New York Times, Oberlin, St. John's University, Northwestern, Yale, Pomona, Harvard, Missouri Baptist, Stanford, Dartmouth, Penn, Columbia, Grinnell, Johns Hopkins, NYU, Brown, North Dakota, McMaster, Maine, British Columbia/Toronto/Chicago, Virginia and Alabama university presses*. He's a Harvard Medical School-trained physician, Stanford professor, healthcare CEO. Currently, he's devoting energy and resources to dealing with climate justice, serving on Climate Action Now's board. Sarnat's belonged to the longest-running U.S. Jewish-Palestinian Dialogue Group. Gerry's been married since 1969 and has three kids, six grandsons — and looks forward to future granddaughters. gerardsarnat.com

Bob McNeil is a writer, editor, cartoonist, and spoken word artist. Flexible Press published his book composed of essays, illustrations, poems, and stories titled *Compositions on Compassion and Other Emotions*. Proceeds from this work fund the National Alliance to End Homelessness.

Emman Usman Shehu is the author of four collections of poetry – *Questions for Big Brother, Open Sesame, Icarus Rising and The River Never Returns*. His poetry has appeared in several journals including *Panoply, Blank Pages, Aayo, Dugwe, Kufena, Dissident Voice, The Shallow Tales Review, Panache, Best New African Poets (BNAP)* series, some anthologies including *Voices from the Fringe, The Anthill Anthology, The Sevage Poetry Flood Collection and Wreaths for a Wayfarer*. Shehu writes across the genres, and is a member of the Abuja Writers Forum (AWF).

Joseph B Pravda was born Brooklyn, NY, graduate of the University of Florida Colleges of Journalism, Law; former U.S. government attorney; on the page/stage/screen/canvas, he storyboards his writing; (created art for UNESCO's DREAM Centers & other international competitions, via http://www.design21sdn.com); 10 pages from his play 'Patsy', involving a fated 'reunion' of JFK Jr. & the oldest daughter of Lee and Marina Oswald, won him a highly competitive place at the Kennedy Center in 2006. Published diversity author via University of Central Florida. Painter/multimedia visual artist with several international exhibits, including

Preface

DONALD TRUMP'S SECOND COMING: Is Democracy Dead, Dying or Alive, An Anthology of North American Writers and African Writers, Vol 4

Some areas of interest:
Did Biden's loose immigration policy and war mongering "deep state" caused the coming back of Donald Trump
Was the American economy and world economy bad under Biden Administration?
Are American institutions strong enough to curtail Donald Trump's want for total control and whimsical policies?
Are the systems of democracy serving the interests of individuals or capital and deep state?
How will Africa and North American countries be adapting to the changing political environment in the USA
Will the USA under Donald Trump continue firming its interests in Africa so as to counteract and balance China's strong influence in Africa?
How will the USA use the sanction regime to push its interests forward, and what effect will the sanctions have on the world's economy, especially on Africa, North America and particularly the US
As the USA move away from its commitments on Climate change, poverty and diseases reduction Aid, politics and international security obligations, what effect will this have and how will the rest of the world cover the gaps
Beyond Donald Trump phenomenon

We invite writers from African continent and North America region to use any literary, visual and academic writings and art to share their stories, poetry, essays, plays, fictions, mixed genres, songs, visual art with us which, and if selected, will be published in this 4rd Volume of African and North American writers, DONALD TRUMP'S SECOND COMING

Our first anthology in this series came out in 2017 as *Africanization and Americanization Anthology, Africa vs North America Vol 1* and our second anthology in this series came out in 2019 as *Nationalism: (Mis)Understanding Donald Trump's Capitalism, Racism, Global Politics, International Trade and Media Wars, Africa Vs North America, Volume2,* and our third anthology focused on the Covid 19 pandemic, *The Trick is to Keep Breathing* in 2022

For prose/mixed genres and plays, 1 piece per writer of not more than 10000 words. For poetry, not more than 3 poems per poet, preferably short poems, for visual art, 5 jpeg digital images of artworks and analysis of the artworks or artist statement.

"I would hurl words into the darkness and wait for an
echo,
and if an echo sounded, no matter how faintly,
I would send other words to tell, to march, to fight,
to create a sense of the hunger for life that gnaws in us all,
to keep alive in our hearts a sense of the inexpressibly
human."
from *Black Boy* by Richard Wright

Eshu's Post-Dated Poem
C. Liegh McInnis

The Berlin Conference is not a history lesson
but a blueprint to ensure that no Wakanda rises
as waves of whiteness wipeout recollections
so that skywalkers cannot return to the pyramids
that function as galactic landmarks
on the journey to our people-lution
while solids learn that liquid and gas
are just rest stops on our odyssey
to the place where we know our names
before they are given to us

But, minds impregnated with fear
will build their own prisons for
Plato's Cave is more comforting
than Delany's ongoing game of
semiotic Three-Card Monte.
Thinking is for those who

accept crucifixion as the sentence
for solving the signs that have been stolen
to craft slick slogans such as the system is the solution
so Ma Bell returns as a four-headed hound
promising infinite G to anyone willing
to accept a SIM card in the neck.
However, Chattanooga Reed has shown us
that even the competitor is owned by the parent company.
Thus, that *Fight to Canada* might as well be a drive
through *Einstein's Intersection* where
poets with no dreams plagiarize Lucretius
to deconstruct the Tower of Babble built by
Isaac and Albert because Gould's warning[1] was ignored
since it's easy to make evolution a religion when
the people masquerading as empiricalists
are just as glutinous as robotic role-playing theologians.

Are credit cards the new Soma
creating the hallucination of citizenship
as we engineer everything from eggs to erections
becoming the Borg colony of consumers
who will eat its own as myopic masterminds of
mediocre machines that mindlessly masturbate
since solving for X and Y is better left
to the ten percent that circumcised their
emotions to become more efficient
builders of plastic perfection?
Yet,

whose Frankenstein's creation was President Agent
Orange?
Whose agent orange was COVID-19?
Whose *Brave New World* is a pile of *Mumbo Jumbo*?
And if COVID Jes Grew,
why did Trumpelstiltskin raid
the Black Knight's treasury
and dismantle the ammunition needed
to slay any dragonous fire-breathing pandemic?[2]
Because America eats more than its young
as pale pirates pillage and plunder the truth
to rape Rainbow Children of their appointment with
destiny.

If it will take carving a crimson peace in an Easter blue sky,
will *Jubilee* be bathed in *Purple Rain* for *Prophets for a
New Day*
to tell us that something does not compute
and that the only thing that is a-u-t-o-matic is
that cells always find a way to divide
even when humans are hell bent
on subtracting themselves.
Thus, Black Kirby creates green Gamas to
illuminate the interstellar path back to the Garden.
Super Sylvester solving string theory
plots Anansi's web across the cosmos
while the devilishly daring deGrasse disentangles
spirals that swirl solutions about stars
pregnant with possibilities remembering supernovas

are mere monuments that we come and go
simultaneously through the shape-shifting matrix.
The crossroad is where
the universe bends at a blues note
signifying in syncopation that
Mojo is a mixture of math and magic
to mesmerize the masses from their mindlessness.

We are all myth-making—
post-modernism is cultural quilting
with borrowed thread and leftover fabric
from a past that has been worn thin into a
future woven with a prism of plum prospects
where Yeshua and Spock can have coffee to
debate the definition of Mr. Data 'cause the
perception of Asimov's Pinocchio is the
projection of what man fears God to be.
So, let's Sankofa our survival
to become sanctified Silver Surfers.
This is what it means to live on the One
and be Funkdafied as our roots are planted
firmly in the fertilizer of the Blues
so that our leaves, branches, and fruit can flower
toward the Sun, enabling us to feed folks
with the fiber they need to blossom beyond
the "Stairway to Heaven" and into the bosom
of the Almighty Benefactor.

So, I'mma take a page from Captain Kirk's log,

commune with a colorful chick, and hope for the best,
thinking that Eshu's coconuts will contain
all the libation that we need for
his postdated payment is still waiting
for us to cross the learning threshold,
but the planetary paradigm is
still to constipated to shift.

[1] *Sephen Jay Gould admonishes the scientific community for its subjective engagement of evolution in "The Evolution of Life on Earth"*
[2] *After Obama doubled the $40 million outlay for epidemiology and laboratory capacity, Trump asked Congress to cut that number to: Zero.*

A Poem For Palestine
Tendai Rinos Mwanaka

This poem rises from the dusty corners of human anguish where hardly nobody cares about when trying to sell war armor
This poem is my scattered notes of death, assembled in a year of death and destruction
This poem cannot starve off death from bombs, bullets, missiles, hunger, starvation, and diseases, inflicted by the angry DOG
In trying to avoid death for the umpteenth time, we keep dying
No resurrection for us, the dead can only vote for the dead
By not dying for the umpteenth time we find the living among unliving
Who can no longer attend to themselves
These are what we call the dead

Standing up for our rights is a crime against the angry DOG
Like spurting water on fire is a crime against the fire
To sleep entire nights on top of our children like mother hen
Protecting our children by our own bodies from pervading death
If a bomb falls on top of the house, the house will not protect us
We hope our bodies will protect our children

You will find us among the broken walls, unearthed roads, shattered and curved schools and clinics
Underneath a mountain of rubble protecting our children from the angry DOG
The bombs are fast descending leaves in windy spaces
And those winds are trying but failing to lift up human guilty
Sheep of clouds hovers all over the skies bloating out our white noise prayers to the above
Day by day, the days are masses of darkness

On 7 October, the sun died, not exploding, not imploding...
Just the light gone, we have lived in darkness forever
This darkness is our wounds refusing to heal
Even after a year of killing, the angry DOG refuses to go like a hungry topography
Starvation, bombs, thirsty, bullets, hunger, displacement... this is how our world has ended!
Not from the big bang or from sinning but from lack of food and water
This is how your own world will end one day when we continue supporting the DOG with bombs and bullets
Our clothes hang on us like we had slipped into them absentmindedly
And now we are trying to put them on, wasting away in this starvation chamber
We now eat tree buck and roots every day to wish away death

In this land the weight of death is the lightness of death
This holocaust is a multiple travels ticket to death
They pushed us from North Gaza to Gaza City, from Gaza city to Dier el Balah, from Dier el Balah to Khan Younis, from Khan Younis to Rafah
Even though all eyes were on Rafah, even though the pharaoh from America said it is a red line
The angry DOG pushed us from Rafah, to Khan Younis, to Dier el Balah, to Gaza City, to North Gaza, to nowhere
Until the angry DOG has managed to wipe out every human animal, he said
Our suitcases are a holocaust story, the rising sun signals a survival dance

The human river has left the streets, only the marauding bombs rule the streets
The city is now only rubble, no markers tells which land belongs to which clan
And the hungry settler across the wire eyes the land of our forefathers
Knowing a year of wear, of war, and of waste will clear for them this human rubble
These are the tourists leading other tourists coveting our land
Calling themselves People of God, chosen people, prophets, angels, gods
Washing their hands in tears of self-righteousness, in denial

Sinwar, Deif, Haniyeh now slaughtered, silenced, quiet in their maternal Aunties' laps
But we will not stop fighting, we will stand in the name of our ancestors
From river to the sea, we must pay with our own blood to dream the Palestinian dream
Of all tribes and races living and working together in this furnace of death
That's all we ever wanted, to be human, to be clothed
That's all we ever wanted, to have a country of our own!

Fill in the dots: of Holocaust Enablers
Tendai Rinos Mwanaka

Evil....... Biden, ...Blinken.....Donaldumb
Stained...Starmer (Sunak), has the knack to kill,.... Scholz
Unscolds..........Netanyahu, ...Gallant
ICJ howls......at Halev, ...Austin ignores ICC
..........Baerbock, ...Cleverly Cameroon is not, Lammy is lame
Baby Napoleon.............Macron, True
Douchebag...Trudeau
Hell's..............................Gates, lying ass Sullivan...
Rubble...Rubio, Leav(e)itT...Gnome Noem guards Us, A...
I don't mean filling in their first names, but say, *'fuck you!'*

I am so scared, Please help me!
Tendai Rinos Mwanaka

The moment we stop running
Bullets, bombs, shrapnel...
Hundreds of them will reach us
Raining down from the skies
That have forgotten about us
They chase after us to drag us
Into the bottomless pits of fire

We are children, we are supposed to be seen
Not heard crying from pits of fire
Our crosses have bleed for decades, centuries
Our venial sins to want a country of our own
Have weighed heavily on our souls
In broken limps, broken souls, broken dreams

"I am only a child
What do you expect me to do, fix it?
I am only 10 years old
I can't even deal with this anymore",
In a language that doesn't have any opposites
Watching trouble falling in heavy sheets
Of fire and smoke from exploding skies
Crying out to a deaf colluding humanity
Is a 10 year old girl
The strength in her voice is thick with fury

"I am scared, please help me", Hind Rajab
5 years old, called out from the world
Now uneven, asymmetrical, dizzy, unstable
She was found 12 days later buried dead under this world

"I am just a kid..." in a hurricane language
Expressing archetypical fear and fury
Yet pretending to be strong, enabling life
Another girl cries out wondering why they deserve this
She is only 6, and for the past year she has been walking
From North Gaza to Rafah, Rafah back to North Gaza
To the West, to East, to North, to South, to South East...

"My legs hurts, I can't walk anymore
My legs are full of blood, they bleed every day
Please help me, I can't take this anymore..."

Poo-spewing Rudy with a Mussolini Flag
Bob McNeil

Migrants
Paris J Smith

The caustic odor of hot tar blew in with the crisp, cool air and made Carlos snuff his nose as he stood in front of the open window. He was a tightly wound fellow in his early-fifties, hair in his beard showing gray strands. A fleshy black mole budded in the crease beside one of his nostrils. The view below the window took in a debris-strewn backyard; patches of weeds sprouted here and there. A rusted-out cooking stove with broken oven doors that hung open sat in a corner beside the fence.

"I finish in moment," called out Leo, the worker, Carlos had hired to do some laborious jobs on his properties. The light-skinned Spanish man lugged a bucket loaded with crumbled plaster and pieces of lathe across the yard to the dumpster in the alley, just outside the backyard gate. His muscular shoulders bulged under his ragged jacket from a lifetime of hard work. But he was a small man, overall.

Carlos nodded in approval to himself. Leo had demonstrated to be a good worker with lots of knowledge about household and construction type things. A couple of extra hundred-dollar bills had motivated him to climb the ladder to the roof and do a patch job.

"How much longer are we going to be here?" said Carlos's wife, Lizabeth, when she strode into the room; new blue jeans enhanced her long legs, hair stood up on her head, one side tinted royal blue. Tall and statuesque, she could truly be referred to as being a *'glamour girl.'*

"Not long," her husband said. "Leo will be done. I'll give him his bread and we can split."

Her disgusted gaze took in the junky room. "That's good to hear."

He frowned. "I know you think buying this building was a bad idea, but just wait and see. We'll rake in a very nice profit. And I figure we might move in one of these units and sell our condo."

She rolled her eyes at him and loomed in the room like some kind of overseer. "We already got three buildings. Don't be so greedy."

"I figure we can damn near triple our investment on this one." He headed over to the table where assorted tools and cans of paint were stored underneath. The room was a shambles; ceiling fallen, walls busted, pieces of broken fixtures and furniture lying about. He picked up a hammer and banged it down, mindlessly, on the tabletop.

She sneered and kicked a piece of wood away from her foot. "Sometimes I don't get where you're coming from." Then the inflection in her voice softened a bit. "And I don't like this Leo character you got working around here, letting him live in the basement with a woman. And I really can't stand her."

Carlos plumbed in his pants pocket and came up with a roll of cash, new bills folded. "You know, he's one of the migrant people. Remember how he almost cried that night, right here in this room sitting on the floor, when he told us about how he came here to this country with his wife from some small town in Venezuela; walked most of the way. Says they got robbed somewhere in Guatemala."

"I don't know if I believe that story," Lizabeth said. "That new crazy house president we got is having migrants rounded up and deported. We might could get in trouble having those illegals here."

Carlos counted out a hundred-and-fifty bucks and laid it on the table; returned the rest of the wad to his pocket.

"Well, I guess you and your friends are glad to hear that," he said. "You always talked bitterly against the migrants."

"Damn right. Those people come here to this country and get taken care of by the government, and given a place to stay and food to eat, while Americans are living on the streets. It's not right, Carlos. You know it's not right. It's not fair. Some of those people are criminals. And look at you, hiring that guy Leo and paying him with cash. You're involving us in an illicit enterprise."

"Life can be a dirty business," he said, picking up the bills he'd counted out.

"That's right, Carlos. A very dirty business."

He flashed his wife a tepid smile. "If I'd hired somebody else, maybe one of the Mexican guys, they would've hit me up for three times as much money. That roofer, Hardaman, wanted twelve-hundred for that patch job, but Leo took care of it and I gave him two. I'm trying to cut corners and make a profit, Lizabeth. And besides, Leo's a married man. You've been around his wife, Rosa. They're nice people."

She ground her shoe heel angrily into the floor and eased closer to him. "Yeah. How do you know if they're really married? And what difference does it make if they're married or not? She's nothing but a drunk, slinking around here twitching her tight ass. She won't look me in the eye. I know where she's coming from. And I know you, Carlos. You done probably hit on her for some damned pussy. I see how you be sneaking little looks at her, like the other day for instance when we were all standing in front of the building. Your dick was hard. I saw it bulging in your pants."

"Hush your mouth, woman. You're having hallucinations. I don't be looking at Rosa." He glowered at his old lady just as a strong gust raged in through the open window. The tar smell had tailed off. His wife got on his nerves when she came out of her jealous bag, quite unnecessarily in this instance, because he hadn't entertained any serious romantic thoughts about the migrant woman. Lizabeth had caught him in bed with one of her girlfriends a couple of years ago and she still held that indiscretion against him.

He stepped to the window and looked out. Leo was securing the padlock on the backyard gate. The migrant turned and looked back at the building and threw his hand up when he saw Carlos at the window.

"Okay, let's get on the road," Carlos said, turning to his wife and giving her the "go" sign with his thumb.

They left out of the second-floor flat and she hit the stairs ahead of him, treading carefully over pieces of rubbish. The

31

main level was also a topsy-turvy wreck. A child's bent up tricycle sat in the midst of some broken pieces of linoleum; exposed wiring hung from the walls. They walked through to the kitchen and finally out the back door into the yard where Leo stood by the broken stairs waiting for them.

"All done, Senor Carlos," the man said. His tawny complexion looked dusty white from the plaster he'd worked with for the greater part of the day. The left side of his mouth was turned down, as though he'd suffered a stroke.

Lizabeth lingered in the background while Carlos handed Leo the cash.

"Now I go get chicken," Leo said. "Rosa love fried chicken they sell at place in next block."

"That's good," Carlos said. "I see you picked up a box of food from the church the other day."

Leo's expression clouded over. "Something in church food make Rosa sick. She puke after she eat."

"That's too bad," Carlos said. "I thought the food pantry gave out good stuff."

Leo shrugged.

"You can start work a little later tomorrow," Carlos informed. "I need to buy some materials at the store."

"Okay. You're boss." The worker nodded, and smiled politely at Lizabeth, then headed toward the front of the building and the street.

"I don't like that man," Lizabeth said in a hushed tone, giving her husband a sinister glare. "He'll come back with the chicken, but he's also going to bring vodka and beer for that funky woman of his."

Carlos sighed exasperatedly. "Don't be like that. Leo and Rosa are just poor. And when you look at me and you, we're doing the same things they do, and what most people do. But we drink more expensive brands of alcohol and we live in a comfortable crib. Remember, we were poor once upon a time. But opportunities came our way and we made the right moves. And believe me when I tell you, Leo is very grateful to us. Remember, him and his wife were staying in a shelter set up by the City and I hired him to work for me, and let them crash in the basement. His wife got beat up really bad by a bunch of young broads in that place where they were staying. But I've told you this before."

"You should've left them in the shelter," Lizabeth replied. "And I told you that before. Damned ICE agents are out there looking for people like them to deport from this country. We might could get in trouble for helping them. And you know those government bastards would love to hassle some black people like us. It's best to do the right thing and don't mess with Uncle Sam."

"You're just paranoid," Carlos declared. "Uncle Sam?? I haven't heard that term in years. But let me tell you: I've seen black dudes who were ICE agents."

They headed along the same narrow gangway route Leo had taken by the side of the building to the front street. No one was about. A few cars were parked at the curbs; the bare branches of the elm trees rustled whisper-like in the gentle wind.

"Where'd you park?" he asked.

She pointed up the street to where their beige Chevy sat next to a full litter basket.

They walked in silence to the car. She was about to get in on the driver's side, but he took hold of the door when she opened it. "That's cool, you drive," she said, and handed him the ignition key.

"You shouldn't get bent out of shape because I hired Leo," he said when they were both sitting in the front seat with their safety belts on. He started the engine and the heater.

"We worked hard and built up our little real estate empire," she went on. "I'd hate to see our efforts get shaded by some damned migrants." She opened the glove compartment hatch and took out a silver-colored flask. Screwed off the cap and raised the vessel to her mouth. Licked her lips when she was done drinking and passed the container to her husband.

After one sip, he grimaced and handed the flask back to her. "Yuck. I can't stand that Remy Martin." He slipped the car into gear and they journeyed out; passed by Leo as he walked toward the chicken shack in the next block. The Spanish man didn't notice them.

"Illegals are being rounded up and shipped out of this country," Lizabeth remarked. Her blue-tinted hair and smeared on bright red lipstick made her look like a carnival character when she glinted a derisive smile. "It's best for us and better for Leo and people like him. They don't need to be here."

"You shouldn't be such a jerk," Carlos countered. "Those people were allowed in through the open border. Some, like Leo and his wife, were shipped up here to Chicago, a sanctuary city. And the use-to-be Mayor sounded proud when she used that term *sanctuary city*. Those migrants didn't ask to be sent here. That governor down there in Texas, or somewhere, did that shit. But could you blame him? Loads of those people were crossing that border every day. Now that they've been housed and fed and can walk the streets, they're suddenly persona non grata and they're being hunted down. I saw on TV how they had migrant men chained up and marched into cells, like they're the worst criminals in the world. And Leo is no criminal. I'm sorry. There's something really wrong with that deportation picture. And the way I see the government doing people is creating a whole new set of poor and homeless waifs in the world."

She chuckled. "You sound like a damned communist. And believe this: more people here think like me than they think like you."

"Lizabeth, you don't even sound like a human being."

"Fuck you, Carlos."

He watched Leo enter the fast-food joint located inside a corner storefront. Leo was doing what many men do, spending his money to please a female. But there was something different about him because he was who he was where he was. Sometimes Carlos thought that the migrants might be the first wave of the change that was inevitably going to come to the ways of life for many. He'd heard it proposed by fantasists: Why have borders in the first place? There was only one race of people on the planet: the human race. Was there a master manipulator at work, and the migrants were its minions? What was the plan for the Americas?

Carlos and Lizabeth resided in a second-floor condo, in a red-brick six-flat building, in a bourgeois world, in a neighborhood just a block from the lake front. It cost them two-thousand bucks per month to stay there where the common lobby was always clean, the fixtures modern, a designated parking space located on the side of the building. He preferred that they didn't live on one of their own properties, at least for a while. He wanted to remain aloof and just collect money from his tenants; get to know the landlord business. That was why Carlos cut corners whenever he could. Expenses were oppressive and rising all the time. Lizabeth brought in good money from her barmaid hustle, and he drove a school bus part-time. Their initial shaky loan that got them started in the property restoration owning business had been approved because Lizabeth's cousin worked as an officer at their bank.

They spent the evening loafing around the flat. The rear dining room transformed into an exotic veranda where vines wound round the table legs and plants grew tall in pots and elongated planters; lights were soft and the fragrance of peppermint tinged the air. Lizabeth lolled on the sofa while Carlos sat in an armchair.

"I wish you hadn't hired that Leo," she said. "And he had to bring along that sorry ass woman."

"Why're you bringing that issue up again?"

"The whole thing about those migrants bugs me. Why're they here?"

"They're not here where we are now," he said. "You shouldn't even be bringing up that subject when we're at our home."

"Oh, yeah? Well, I know I've worked hard all my life, and you have too, Carlos. You did ten years driving and delivering for that parcel company; threw your back out and had to have surgery. And let me tell you, I've gotten so I can't stand this barmaid business. Drunken men always want to flirt and talk under my clothes. Yeah. The tips are fabulous, but believe me when I tell you, hosting those bars and tables is a grind. I'm ready to work in an office again.

These capitalists have exploited us both, and our people before us even worse. That's why I feel how I feel about those migrants being here. They should stay in their own country and start a revolution instead of running away. Dr. King didn't run. He got things organized and battled these racists and segregationists and affected changes here in this country. Castro didn't run. Mandela didn't run. And you know, my Uncle Bishop was in SNCC when he was a young man living in Alabama. He's still carrying a scar in his face today from where a cracker hit him with a piece of iron."

She picked up the TV remote and tuned in a news program where the ruins of a Ukrainian city destroyed by war bombs showed in a film clip.

Carlos shook his head. "It's a complex state of affairs confronting us now. All over the world challenges are facing people. Death, doom and destruction prevail."

"Complex my ass," she rebutted. "It looks clear to me. My old folks caught nothing but pure hell living down there in Louisiana and working in them damned fields all their life; taking them old white folks' insults and Jim Crow crap." Antagonism flared in Lizabeth's eyes and her mouth quivered.

He grinned broadly at his wife lying on the sofa across from him and said, "Then we're all in the same boat battling these racists and capitalists." At that moment, he didn't see the circus character in her face, and he wasn't at all sure if he liked the female wearing the mask that made her look like his wife. And he went on. "You always go for the obvious that's set out for you to see and be impressed by. Don't you get it how this government operates? That old orange ogre they put in the White House is getting away with doing all his crap. But I see a serious fix in the game. How was he able to mount all these assaults so quickly? He knew he was going to win. They all knew. And I'm talking about all those hotshots at the top."

After a long silence, Lizabeth spoke up again. "Why was somebody trying to do up Leo's old lady in that shelter? Something is not right about Leo and that so-called wife of his."

Carlos shrugged. "I can't say exactly what happened to his wife. When I saw her the first time, she had a busted lip and a bloody nose."

"I bet the trouble had something to do with her ass," Lizabeth said.

Carlos propped his bare feet up on a hassock. "I doubt that," he countered. "She's a family type of woman."

Lizabeth let out a bellicose laugh and told her husband, "You sound like somebody who was just born yesterday."

"Dearest," he answered. "You always think the worst about people in all situations. But I understand. You can't help but think the way you do because that's the way you are. Evidently, you don't see that Leo and I have an understanding. We're helping each other. He's working for us on the dirt cheap, and I'm paying him and giving him a place to stay with his girl."

Nothing more was said between them for a stretch of time. Carlos sat and listened to the background hum of the city, its roaring vehicles and machines mingling with croaks, cat screeches and occasional barking dogs. At one time in the days' past, he'd heard music in the air, but not anymore.

"Seems like there's still lots of work to do in this place," Lizabeth said, breaking the silence.

"It looks that way," Carlos replied. "I'll probably have to bring in one more guy to get the job done."

"Is that so? Well, don't hire no more of those damned illegals. It's plenty full-fledged Americans out here who need work. That Mexican fellow, Estrada, you brought in last month to fix the plumbing at the condo did a damned good job."

Carlos pouted and shifted around in the chair. "Yeah. But Estrada wants to be paid at least standard wages."

Lizabeth reached down under the sofa and came up with a small wooden box which she opened and took out a white envelope.

"What's that?" he asked.

"Some weed."

"Where'd you get it? Our regular man told me he was out, and wouldn't have any weed until next week."

She didn't answer while she extracted a rolled joint from the envelope. Used a lighter that lay on the table to fire up the stick. Took a long drag and puffed out the smoke.

"I bet you bought the stuff from that kid who hangs out on the corner sometimes outside the tire shop," he said.

She threw up her hand dismissively and passed him the smoldering joint.

"You hypocrite," he accused, taking the weed. "That kid is one of the migrants. He's nothing but a hoodlum."

"That's alright," she warned. "I'll still hand his migrant ass over to ICE in a hot minute, if it comes to that. I heard there's a cash reward of some hundreds of dollars if you turn one of those bastards in. I don't know how true that is."

"You're sickening, Lizabeth." He took a pull on the joint and coughed.

"Didn't you say this migrant stuff is dirty business?" she told him.

"I said *life* can be a dirty business." He passed the joint back to her.

"Well, this is life," she said. "And anyway: fuck them damned immigrants. And look at your ass, smoking the reefer, too."

"Stop it, Lizabeth."

For the remainder of the evening, the couple relaxed in their condo and indulged in food and drink and watched a movie on the streaming service they subscribed to. There was no more mention of migrants or real estate ventures. When Lizabeth turned in for the night, Carlos delved into his passions; he was putting together an intricate jigsaw puzzle based on astrological signs, and when he was through with that activity, he picked up his history books. His current interest focused on the Russian Revolution and the Marxist ideals put forth by Lenin.

That next morning, Carlos left his wife stretched out naked in bed sleeping and snoring. He gave her a gentle kiss on her backside and muttered, "I love you, honey." Stepped out into a chill when he departed from the flat. A brilliant sun dominated a cloudless sky while he headed in his car for the construction supply store. The crowd of men that usually hung around the parking lot entrance, mostly speaking Spanish, was diminished, he presumed, because the immigration officers were showing up and arresting guys who might be illegal. He parked and went inside the huge store. Moving quickly along the aisles, he purchased several bags of plaster and some nails. A chubby girl with knock-knees and a high ass checked him out at the register. He pushed his load on a flatbed cart to his ride.

The drive to his property went quickly as he whizzed through red lights and STOP signs at isolated intersections. The city vista appeared gray, except for the white lines drawn as guides on the street surfaces. He parked his car in the alley behind the building and went to the basement door and knocked, intending to enlist Leo's brawn to bring in the heavy bags of plaster. Then he realized how fearful the migrant people probably were because of on-going ICE sweeps, and he knocked again and called out, "Hey, it's Carlos."

Presently, the door opened and a healthy-looking woman stood there in the dimness staring at him with muggy eyes. She was Leo's wife, Rosa. Her stringy hair was an auburn color, massive breasts filled the front of her flannel gown, soggy back side was stuffed into some sweat pants. He'd been in her company a few times before and he'd picked up some kind of vibe from her.

"Where's your husband?" he asked.

"Sleeping," she replied, timidly.

Carlos didn't feel the need to be particularly polite. He owned the property and could do as he pleased. So, he pushed past the woman and headed into an adjacent space where he found Leo stretched out in his dirty underwear on a stained mattress. The man's eyes were closed. Plastic bags stuffed full of clothes and junk were stashed away in a corner. The brick walls were flaky, and a make-shift lamp had been put together using a naked bulb dangling from an exposed fixture in the ceiling. An ancient-looking electric heater was also plugged in and radiated comforting warmth.

Carlos glanced around when he heard footsteps enter the room. Rosa, the wife, had come in.

"Leo, he very tired," the woman said, her expression strained, pimples and abrasions dotted her light-colored skin. "He work so much, and I work so much. But he get all the hard work. Everyone hate each other where we come from, and that's because nobody's life get better."

Carlos nodded, and shouted, "Come on, Leo. You got plastering to do."

The wife's tale of woe made Carlos feel sympathetic toward Leo and Rosa as migrants, but he'd heard their complaints before, and he still didn't fully understand why they were stultified in their unique predicament. Why had they taken such great risks to get into the United States? And why so many at one time? They weren't refugees fleeing bombs and terror; maybe they were a different kind of refugee, on the run fun from poverty and ruling class domination. But none of that should've concerned him.

And just then, the Venezuelan sat up and groaned, eyes still shut, and let out a resonant fart.

"Okay, boss. I put on my clothes."

Carlos and Rosa returned to the first room where it wasn't so warm.

She eased close to Carlos and whispered, "When we have date?"

He reached and squeezed her titty nipple through the flannel gown. Yeah, she was a hot woman, and Lizabeth had been right when she accused him of having been aroused by Rosa, but she was married, and he was married.

And right then they stepped away from each other when Leo emerged from the adjacent space, chest rattling with a phlegmy cough; complexion sickly sallow.

"He always like this when he first start day," Rosa said, sounding desperately defensive. "But he's not sick."

Then Leo cut in with, "That's right, Senor Carlos. I be better quick."

Carlos led the way to the car so that Leo could handle the sacks of plaster. The coughing subsided and color returned to the laborer's face after he moved around in the fresh air. His primary task for the day was to continue with the plastering. He went to the room where his work awaited him; moved his ladder and gathered up his implements.

Carlos hung around for a short time and engaged the fellow in chitchat. He'd spoken in close quarters with the migrant before, but they were still strangers to each other.

"Where'd you learn English?" Carlos asked when they were together in the room where the work was to be done.

"I learn English in school."

"Were you a good student?"

He shook his head. "No. Not so good. But I know how to do things."

"Is that how you made a living in Venezuela?"

"Si, Senor. I work hard, but life not good there. Rosa and me went to same school when we were children. Then for a long time we didn't see each other, but then we start seeing each other again, and we fall in love. Si? Like I told you other time we talk, crime and murder all the time where we come from. I work when I could find work, but not so much. Man named Ramos say he have set-up for us here in the United States. Show me pictures on his phone. I give him my last money, two-thousand dollars. But there was no set-up when we got here. You are set-up, Senor Carlos." And he laughed. And Carlos laughed, too.

Leo went about putting his work setting in order, laying down drop cloths and opening a bag of plaster. "Your President talks very mean about my people," he said. "Myself and my woman only have good intentions when we come to this country. But we don't have the right papers. To get here, we walk through jungles, and across mountains and rivers. Snakes, animals and robbers attack us. I see people die and bodies be left on the trails."

And Carlos told him, "Well, keep your chin up. Things can only get better."

Leo laughed and gave his benefactor a sarcastic wink when he picked up his mud pan and headed for the kitchen and the sink.

Carlos felt embarrassed because his words of encouragement had actually sounded like a whimsical wisecrack. How could the Spanish migrant's life evolve into something better under present circumstances? Armed government agents were prowling the streets, on the lookout for his kind. They wanted to detain him and boot him out of the country, destroy his dream and reduce his perilous journey into a wasted effort. And how solid was Leo's love life with Rosa? The woman showed moral looseness. Did Leo see it?

Carlos left the building and headed home. If Lizabeth was still in bed, he intended to get back in there with her. She was the woman he really loved; truly his soul mate. The sex he had with one of her friends, and got caught in the act, had been his lust getting the better of him while he was full of liquor and cocaine. No way could he justify what he'd done. But Lizabeth understood her man's passions, and he knew she wanted to keep him, as her man, no matter what. They'd been together for eleven years, married for eight. Now, he'd got out of line when he fondled Rosa's breast, but that was as far as he was going with her. He didn't particularly care for the way she looked in the face, pimply and beady-eyed. She'd hit on him slyly about them having a date, and he brushed her off. He understood that any such encounter with a female such as Rosa, or with any kind of woman for that matter, would entail him coming up with money or something of material value to sweeten the tryst. But then gremlin-like thoughts came to mind and he considered the possibility of taking advantage of the migrant woman, since he was already exploiting her man, and she'd let him know where she was coming from when she proposed that they have a date. Then quickly, he dismissed the adulterous notion from his thoughts. Lizabeth's breast was what he liked.

Carlos arrived at the condo and found his wife up and dressed, pouring her second cup of brandy-spiked coffee, ready to hit the streets. She wore flare-bottom pants and a black leather jacket; hair was tied in a ball on her head, the blue wisps piled at the top. He would've rather spent some time in bed with Lizabeth, but she seemed hopped up to get going...somewhere. So, he followed her lead and they ventured out.

For the better part of the day, they just frittered away the hours, hanging out in up-scale lounges where the lights were low and the background music smooth. They were always kissing and feeling on each other. Enjoyed a fabulous buffet brunch at a Northside bistro where the walls were decorated with black and white photos of famous musicians and night club performers from many years ago. Carlos knew how to turn on the charm and Lizabeth could be alluring. They considered themselves to be living large and enjoying some of the finer things in life. While cruising through the outskirts of Downtown, they got slowed down in traffic by a large number of people milling about, holding up signs that expressed solidarity for the Palestinians being wiped out by the Israelis.

"That's part of what I mean when I say the world is so complex," Carlos said. And he had to slow the car when a couple of young women stepped out into the street waving their placards. One of the girls had long flaxen-colored hair; her companion wore military fatigues. Policemen wearing helmets moved in and pushed the demonstrators back onto the curb.

"Looks like a fresh batch of poor migrants is being created over there in Gaza," Lizabeth said.

"My goodness, woman," Carlos countered. "You have no sympathy for the underdogs in this world."

"Why should I have sympathy? I'm an underdog myself."

He laughed. "Not hardly, my dear. You got plenty going for yourself in this good old USA. We both do. That's why all these migrants are here. They want what you and me got – or what they think we got."

They headed back to the Southside, and for a brief interlude, they sat in the car by the lakefront with the motor and heater running and blew a joint. Outside, the air felt chilly; sky was clear.

"Don't you think we deserve to enjoy this beauty?" Lizabeth said in a pensive tenor, breaking a silence that kindled between them and lingered. With her open hand, she swept the lakefront scene that spread out beyond the car's windshield, the lofty trees, and the gigantic limestone rocks that held back the expanse of water.

"We earned what we have in this world," he said. "I mean the material things, the money. All the natural beauty that abounds on this Earth is for each and every one of us to partake of and enjoy."

She gave him an extended, penetrating stare with glistening eyes, and lapped her lips. Then she said to him, most nonchalantly, "I want to suck your dick." And that was what she did right then and there in the front seat of the car; made him holler when his cookie came.

When their fun day wound down and the sun faded, they made the rounds checking on their properties: a yellow-brick three-flat; a six-unit with wide picture windows in the front; a multi-apartment court way where a marble bird bath sat in the front yard, and lastly the two-flat they'd recently acquired where Leo was presently working on the renovation. Carlos did the driving and parked on the street in front of the building behind another vehicle, a white cargo van already sitting there. "I don't like the looks of this," he said when he noticed an official style decal emblazoned on the back door of the van. He gave the vicinity an across-the-board visual scan. Nothing else looked to be out of the ordinary.

"What's up?" Lizabeth said, obviously sensing her husband's wariness.

"I'm not sure." Carlos opened the car door and stepped out. The street was empty and the night tide was settling in. He looked up at the building. All was dark, and that seemed unusual because Leo usually kept lights burning in the rooms where he worked.

Lizabeth climbed out of the car and looked around, suspiciously. Pointed to the emblem on the van's back door. "That's the INS," she said in a bitter sounding voice. "They'll put an end to the trouble here."

"Just be cool," Carlos said.

And right then a quartet of armed men wearing uniforms clambered out from the front door of the building, voices low. They were all white guys and appeared to be in good shape. One fellow looked like the Incredible Hulk, skin milky-colored instead of pea green, massive arms and shoulders lumpy inside his shirt; bottom jaw hung like a pouch beneath his flabby lips. He fired a glance at Carlos and Lizabeth and paused while the other men got inside the van.

The hulking uniformed fellow pointed at Carlos and spoke sharply in a rapid-fire voice, "You got something to do with this property?"

For a moment, Carlos and his wife glowered at one another.

"I own this building," Carlos said.

"We're with Immigration," the big guy explained. "We have reason to believe illegal aliens are staying here."

"No one lives here. I don't know anything about illegal aliens. We're rehabbing the place and I hire American and legal workers. Sometimes Mexican or Black, maybe Polish or Russian."

"That makes you a DEI employer," the big guy remarked, cynically.

A chill made Carlos quake. He looked at his wife standing by, her blue hair ruffled by the wind. Hopefully, she would remain quiet.

"I just want to get this rehab job done," Carlos replied.

'Okay," said the big officer. "It would be in your best interests to call us if you get any of those migrants snooping around here. They're always looking for some kind help or a handout. And they'll work for cheap." He gave Carlos a facetious wink.

"I can dig it," Carlos agreed, forcing a smile.

The big guy climbed into the van with the rest of the agents and the vehicle rolled away.

"What the hell was that?" Carlos tolled.

"Just what it looked like," Lizabeth said. "See there. I warned you about hiring that fucking migrant."

"Evidently, they didn't find him or Rosa. But what brought them here?"

"They went inside the building, Carlos. They meant sure enough business, ready to bust some heads if they had to."

Carlos looked up at the unlit structure. Where had Leo and Rosa disappeared to? Or had they managed to hide somewhere inside? His stomach was in a tumult. Conflict with the authorities had to be avoided. He and Lizabeth entered the building. A small flashlight he took out of his pocket gave off a powerfully bright beam as they searched the rubbish-cluttered apartments.

"Let's check the basement," Carlos said.

Lizabeth agreed. Then she assumed a commanding stance and said, "But first I want to suck your dick some more."

"My goodness, Lizzy. Now's not the time for that."

She snickered. "It's always time for me to get some of you."

He made a goofy face at her. "Your ass stays hot."

And she came back, indignantly, "That's why you married me."

He snickered.

And right then something made a bumping noise somewhere close by. Carlos had let his crotch zipper down, but quickly zipped it back up. "Who's there?" he called out, pointing the light in the direction where the sound came from.

"It's me, Senor," answered a familiar male voice.

Leo stepped out into the light; a shadow assuming human animation.

"What's going on here?" Carlos asked.

"ICE come and I hide, Senor Carlos. I see van from window and I know it's them, but they don't see me. I turn lights off and hide." '

"What about your wife? Where is she?"

"Rosa gone to do day labor. Work at factory to get paid. I'm glad she wasn't here when ICE come."

"Ain't this a blip," Lizabeth cut in.

Carlos intercepted his wife's antipathy. "Don't start, Lizzy. Please. This is some serious business going down here."

"Damn right it's serious," she came back. "I wouldn't be surprised to find out this man is working for the cartels." She glared and gestured forcefully at Leo. "He might be with the gangs they be talking about."

The migrant assumed a hang dog posture, head lowered.

"He's no drug smuggler, and no gang thug either" Carlos said.

"How the hell do you know what he is?"

"Why you want to act ignorant, Lizabeth?"

"You're wrong, Carlos. I'm not being ignorant at all."

Leo stood there, head lowered, eyes on the floor. Carlos figured that the migrant man knew he had better stand there and absorb Lizabeth's mouthy abuse. Any aggression he might come back on her with would surely stir her husband into action. And that was how Carlos really felt about his girl. No one had better mess with her for any reason. But she was putting him in an awkward position.

Right then a female voice and the emergence of Rosa into the apartment captured everyone's attention. She wore a pink coat that was too big for her, and her face looked heavily made-up. Her flushed complexion Carlos had seen before in the visages of the alcoholics who'd passed through his life over the years.

"Rosa, ICE was here," Leo blurted out. "I hid and they didn't find me. I think they'll be back."

"Somehow ICE found out you all be hanging around here," Carlos said. "Some nosy busybody must've seen you coming and going." He gave Rosa an up and down scan. No, he didn't want her for her femaleness. The garish red lipstick and tiny hairs that populated the skin under her chin turned him off. But those imperfections had been there all time. Now he noticed them more than before.

He looked at Lizabeth standing there, gloating.

Leo had more to say. "Maybe it better if I surrender to ICE. I get free ride back to Venezuela. There I be poor, just like I'm poor here, but I don't have to be flunky, like I be here with you, Senor Carlos."

He watched the migrant man's body snap into a viable personage, a prideful human being with a sense of himself. The hang dog expression changed to something confrontational. Was he going to have to fight Leo?

"You can't mean what you say," Carlos said. "You went through some heavy changes to get here to the United States. And there's no telling where you'll wind up once you fall into ICE's hands. They're shipping illegals like you down there to that prison at Guantanamo Bay, Cuba. And even people who are legal are being snatched. That's what I hear. America used to stand for righteousness in this world, but not anymore. Tyranny rules from all corners of the globe now."

"If he said he wants to surrender, he means it," Lizabeth interjected, sharply. "Accept it. If he wants to give up, that's his business. He's a grown man."

"I don't want to go back to Venezuela," Rosa declared, raising her voice, a fierce expression contorting her face.

"She talk crazy," Leo said. "She go where I go."

Carlos felt sorry: sorry for the way the migrants were being treated by the government, sorry for having involved his life with theirs, sorry that he knew about all the injustice in the world. And perhaps he felt ashamed. But he had no reason to feel that way. The ball of confusion that confronted all of them had been created by anonymous men sitting in high places.

"Why don't you and Rosa call it an early night?" Carlos said, hoping his voice might dispel some of the foreboding that faced the migrant couple. "Hide yourselves in the basement and keep quiet. We'll have to have figure something out. You're probably right. Those immigration law bastards will be back." And Carlos thought about why he spoke despairingly about the ICE men. They weren't looking for him. But by him being an AfroAmerican man, he carried an inherent distrust and dislike for all the kinds of cops.

The migrant couple did as Carlos suggested and retired to their basement space; set some pieces of broken furniture in front of the door. Carlos and Lizabeth lingered in the upstairs apartment and shared a joint in the darkness. The only light was what filtered in through the window from the moon and the streetlamps.

"Those ICE agents are working off a tip," Carlos said. "That was no random raid they made here earlier. There's no migrant shelter in this neighborhood, and we don't see Immigration agents snooping around." He peered out the window at the deserted street. Lights burned in the neighboring buildings. For an instant he felt as though he existed in some otherworldly universe, like in a land of enchantment.

"It's best those migrant people be gone," Lizabeth grumbled. "That Rosa bitch is nothing but a drunken slut."

He watched a battered pick-up truck roll and rattle past the building, one of its tail lights not burning. The vehicle belonged to an elderly gentleman named Mr. Copland, whom he'd hired a few days ago to haul away some trash. Bad words had been spoken by Mr. Copland about foreigners taking jobs, and he'd given Leo a nasty look when the two of them loaded the truck.

Carlos finally reacted to his wife's condemnation of the migrant woman. "Rosa's just poor, and has lived a hard life."

"That might be true," Lizabeth admitted. "But she needs to live her poor life in Venezuela, or where ever the hell she comes from. We got enough drunken bitches here in this country already. I'm here to tell you, Carlos, that Rosa bitch is nothing but a tramp. I don't want that kind of female staying on our property."

It was moments such as these when he didn't like his wife very much. But he still loved her despite the reproachful comments about the migrants that spewed like a poisoned spring from her mouth. She'd always acted hardnosed that way, despairing in attitude to those who happened to be less fortunate than what she happened to be.

"We may as well head to the crib," Carlos said.

"I guess so," Lizabeth agreed. "But let's hang for a few minutes longer. Those ICE cops should be back."

He gave her an inquisitive stare. "What's with you wanting to wait for those guys? And how do you know they'll be back?"

"They missed their mark when they were here before. This time I'll make sure they do what they're supposed to do."

"I don't like the way you're talking, Lizzy. Did you drop a dime on Leo? You been sneaking and calling those ICE people?"

She moved to the window when the sound of a vehicle stopped outside the building. "Yeah. I called them this time while you wasn't paying attention. Those officers that came the first time were acting on a call I made last week."

Carlos kept a perplexed stare leveled at his wife, a pretty woman, a sensual woman, the only woman he wanted to be with. But she'd done the Devil's work when she informed on Leo and Rosa. And he didn't like that at all.

"They're here," she said, gleefully, turning away from the window. "I'm going to show them where those rats are hiding in the basement."

Carlos felt stunned. "How could you do such a thing, Lizabeth? Leo and his wife haven't wronged us any kind of way. The work he's doing here is saving us thousands."

"What you're talking about justifies nothing. Why should I approve of those people being here?"

He pointed accusingly at his wife, the glow from his flashlight giving her a form he could see in the otherwise darkened room. "You talk a lot of corny stuff," he said. "You throw around the names of some true revolutionary icons. I know Mandela wouldn't dig your way of thinking. And your actions have done more to show how you're an indecent human being."

She pointed back at him and took up a defiant stance. "I told you I don't like those people, and I especially don't like that Rosa bitch."

Then came the sound of clomping footsteps approaching on the stairs.

"It's for the best they're gone from here," Lizabeth proclaimed. "I'm just as much an owner of this property as you are. It says so on paper at City Hall. I can call some shots and have those illegals removed."

Four ICE agents barged into the room, brandishing flashlights. Certainly, a different squad from those who'd been there before. They looked mean, disheveled and tired. Again, an all-white crew.

One of the agents, a slinky man with dirty red hair sprouting from under his cap, said to Lizabeth, "You got something for us this time?"

"I sure do."

Carlos stood by absolutely flabbergasted, not sure what to do or say or believe.

"Follow me to the basement," she said, motioning to the officers, then giving her husband an impudent glare.

Lizabeth directed the agents to the underground room where Leo and Rosa were holed up. Carlos came right along and never opened his mouth in protest. He felt like a punk because he didn't challenge the lawmen's authority over him and his property. The head officer banged on the basement room's door and announced their official presence, then a couple of the other guys kicked open the door and all four men stormed into the room to find the migrants seated side by side on a floor blanket, candle sitting in front of them burning and flickering, casting a glow on their woeful looking faces that was almost mystical. Leo offered no resistance when his hands were zip-tied behind his back and he was stood against the wall, but Rosa raised all manner of hell, kicking and clawing, and cursing in Spanish. Carlos felt aghast. He hadn't pegged Rosa as being the fighting type, but she came on ferociously. Her fire got doused when she spit in one of the agent's faces, and that white man hauled off and bashed the living shit out of her, knocked her lips crooked and made her bite her tongue and bring on blood. Dropping to her knees, she looked around in a daze. And Leo had to stand there and watch his wife get fired on.

Carlos choked up when Leo broke down in pitiful tears and begged, "Don't hit her no more, Senor. Please don't hurt her."

Lizabeth looked on in mild astonishment, and Carlos knew instantly what was on her mind: the brutality against Rosa had shocked and frightened her. She liked to come on like a tough dame, but violence freaked her out. The agents changed up their roles. The fellow that hit Rosa moved away and another man stepped in and zip-tied her wrists, told her, "You'll behave yourself now. And believe this. I hit harder than the other fellow does."

Carlos was sure the ICE men would give him a hard time, but he turned out to be wrong about that. No one even asked his name. They loaded Leo and Rosa into back of the van, and a couple of guys got in the cab. The red-haired leader of the troop, along with the man who'd hit Rosa, stood with Carlos and Lizabeth out front of the building.

"You did the right thing calling us," said the mantis-like commanding ICE man directly to Lizabeth. "Those people should've never been here in this country in the first place. There're more of them that need to be rounded up, and believe me when I tell you they will be,"

"Yeah. My husband..." she began.

But the officer cut her off. "No need to explain anything to me. Mission accomplished. We got who we came here to get, thanks to you." Then he looked at Carlos. "You got to watch who you hire these days. But everyone and everything is so damned expensive. It's hard to come out on top." He gave Carlos a final sneer and smiled with a nod at Lizabeth.

"I don't want to go back in that building," Lizabeth said as the ICE men sped away in their van with Leo and Rosa locked up inside while the black sedan followed directly behind.

"I can't believe you did some lowdown shit like that," Carlos chastised.

"What I did needed to be done."

"But why, Lizzy?"

She pawed at the ground with the toe of her shoe, like a prize pony might do, and said, emphatically "The bitch wanted to fuck you, nigga."

He went silent and stared in disbelief at Lizabeth. And at that same moment he almost fell into a swoon, because he genuinely loved her, and it didn't matter what she'd done, although he wished that she hadn't done it. But her feelings and reasoning were justified. Rosa had asked him slyly about them having a date, and he'd squeezed her titty nipple. On a few occasions when he'd been in the woman's presence, he'd got hard for her. And he knew all along that Rosa understood Lizabeth's resentment of her.

With Carlos driving the car, they headed toward their residence where the living for them was easy. A cool night settled in on the city.

"I feel bad about what happened to Leo and Rosa," he lamented.

Lizabeth gave him a dismayed look, and said, while her hand reached across the car seat and gently massaged between his legs, "To hell with them damned people. You'll find another ass rag like that Leo to work for cheap. But no more bitches. And I mean that. Now, stop at the liquor store so we can get some of that imported beer to go along with the steaks I'm going to cook."

The end

Sympathy for Uncle Sam
Bob McNeil

The battlefield of poverty
Abigail George

While Musk has the listening
ear of President Trump
whose ex-model wife
wears pretty dresses
Their son is handsome
I wonder though if he is kind
Their kitchen is made of gold
My father washes the dishes
He says he found
Four generations
Of maggots in just that one pot
A star passes
through me
through my palm
through our shared past
through our poverty
through the power of the dish
my father is holding in his right hand
It whirls, pinched,
into the sides of
that gigantic pot
making like a battlefield
calling forth
particles of salt into light.

Yesterday
Abigail George

A void
that is what you
sound like to me now
The rain
pours down
The kettle boils
I no longer
carry the weight
of your love
I am ill
My sickness is undefined
I wake up
the sheets are damp
The bed is wet
with my urine
When you telephone
from deep inside Europe
you look at me first
on the screen, on the phone
as if I am invisible,
then when I begin to
speak you blink and
look at me as if I am
an insect, a stain
that will be difficult
to get out, as if I am

something rotten
Then you look away
and eat a piece of steak
with sweet potato chips
what the Americans
call French fries
Je me souviens
One girl said
you're ugly
Another said
your schoolbag smells
like cat pee
And another asked,
do you need to brush your hair
Has my mother
known such Model C pain
or Trump?

When I have a problem with myself, I write really bad poetry
Abigail George

()
Today I am as sad
as the distant sea
It doesn't matter to
my heart for my heart
can block out the sun
while I fry an egg
in butter, oil and grease
while I cook up some bacon
I burn the toast
I confess
these black squares
edges brown and crisp
taste delicious, they remind
me of hell
Do drug addicts go to hell
if they have children?
Will my brother
go to hell or heaven?
He hit me once
slapped me very hard
across my face
My spectacles fell off
and broke
Something inside me fell too

and broke
The sun had a stroke
The moon needed
to be rehabilitated
My hands lost all feeling
I turned the page
Trump trumped my pain
I remembered
when my brother was young
How he looked up to me
How we would
talk late into the night
Now he calls me lesbian
Dyke, you're a stupid dyke
he calls me
You, you man!
but I know it's the drugs
not my brother
Nobody wants you, he says
The magistrate
wouldn't have married you
I wished I was whole again
instead of these
broken parts
I think of the man
who called me beautiful once,
the man I called Husband
the man I was going to marry
but that was years ago

Now I care for my father
and babysit my brother's children
I write for the screen
In the evenings
I draw the curtains
I sit on my bed
I think about the man
how he vanished
like cigarette smoke
in my coffee
my arms quite dead
at my sides
I stare at the wall in the dark
I sit and stare
at the opposite wall
in the dark
Sometimes I will
be in the mood to pray,
or I remember
how I was touched by madness
called mentally ill
rejected by the church, society
immediate family
My sister doesn't talk to me
She is a White woman now
European
Is there any beauty
in this poem?
This is an ugly poem

made of glass
This is a poem
that hurts your head
that's a grievance
All I see is my hurt
my brown colour, my pain
and this scar tissue
The garden makes it go away
It stops my tears dead
in their tracks
Now I have the dogs for company
and this sad music
and books
and children that run
into my arms
I have the clouds too
and rain
The years feel like summer now
and my brother's voice
when he holds his daughter
There are dreams in suffering
you know
and stars
My brother is a star
My sister
My mother, my father
and the man
who was so very briefly
in my life

Tomorrow
there will be
black holes
in our souls, consternation
giving way to constellation
I shiver now, blue
I sit on my bed
and open a light beer
thinking of the man
who I thought was a genius
who calls Cambodia
home now
There's a brief history
of time
on my tongue
I swallow
It tastes bitter.

Donald Trump has been president for a month now
Charlie R. Braxton

Donald Trump has been president for a month now, and already his constituents are complaining. Social media is replete with many MAGA supporters who have found themselves negatively affected by Trump's radical dismantling of the U.S. government's bureaucracy. According to a report by NPR, thousands of federal employees at various agencies such as Veterans Affairs, Energy, and Education departments have been devastated by Trump. Also, federal entities such as the Pentagon and the Department of Housing and Urban Development are preparing for massive budget cuts and staff lay-offs. Many MAGA supporters throughout the country who work for federal agencies or federally funded programs have found out that Trump's efforts have cost them their jobs, and they aren't feeling it or him.

Trump's poll numbers are below the 50% mark, consistent with his last presidency. Only this time Trump is doing worse than he did the first time.

The latest Gallup Poll has Trump's approval rating standing at 40%, which is down from his first presidency. According to Washington Post reporter Aaron Blake, the President's approval ratings range from 44% to 47% in other polls by organizations such as CNN, Reuters, Quinnipiac University, and the Washington Post-Ipsos polls. All the poll numbers fall below 50%, which isn't good news for Donald Trump.

"President Donald Trump came into office claiming a sweeping and historic mandate, but that was always oversold," writes Blake. He states that the popular vote for Trump was relatively modest; adding that his "honeymoon phase" pales in comparison to every other modern president "not named Trump." This makes him perhaps the most unpopular president in modern times.

Aside from the deep budget cuts and the mass federal firings, there are other factors that make Trump unpopular at the moment.

For example, the shuttering of USAID, a major part of America's soft power used to carry favor with foreign countries, seems unpopular. According to the Post-Ipsos Poll, 59% opposed the move while a mere 38% approved of the idea. That's a difference of 21%.

Americans aren't too happy with Trump's tariffs either. A CNN poll shows that 49% of Americans oppose his tariffs on aluminum and steel with 34%, while a Post-Ipsos poll indicates that nearly 2-to-1 opposition to his 25% tariffs on goods from Mexico and Canada. Around 7 in 10 Americans believe that tariffs generally raise the price of products in the U.S.

Speaking of high prices, the economy is posing quite a problem for the president, who promised that he would whip inflation, and lower the grocery prices as soon as he got in office. At a campaign rally in August Trump said, "Starting on Day 1, we will end inflation and make America affordable again." Thus far, the only thing Trump has done about inflation is blame Joe Biden.

As of this writing, the Bureau of Labor Statistics reports that the consumer price index accelerated a seasonally adjusted 0.5% for the month, putting the annual inflation rate at 3% in February. In other words, inflation is still rising. Add to this the rising cost of food, and gas; things are looking grim for the average American. This is undoubtedly leading to a sharp decline in Trump's approval numbers.

The Post-Ipsos poll indicates that 53% of Americans disapprove of his handling of the economy. That's Trump's worst economic numbers since 2017. Meanwhile, a Reuters poll shows his economic approval at a dismal 39%, Trump's worst rating to date. Apparently, people are very upset about Trump's inability to curb inflation and bring down the price of gas and food.

To be completely fair to Donald Trump, he's only been in office a month, and there's not a lot he can do to curb inflation in that amount of time. Anybody who paid attention in their high school economics class would know that. But I don't think that is the crux of the real issue here.

It's the optics of Trump's cold, hard callousness; his seeming not to give a fuck about the average American's suffering in these hard economic times, which is requiring many Americans to make financial sacrifices to make ends meet. Meanwhile, according to reports, Trump has spent over 25% of his current presidency playing golf, costing taxpayers 10.7 million dollars. Perhaps this is why a CNN Poll says that 62% of the people polled feel like Trump isn't doing enough to reduce prices, and 51% of Republicans who CNN polled feel the same way.

Polls also indicate that people are equally displeased at Trump's cozy relationship with billionaire tech bro Elon Musk.

Musk is a special advisor to the president and heads Trump's newly formed Department of Government Efficiency (DOGE). Trump has given DOGE carte blanche to examine the records of every governmental department for efficiency and waste and make whatever changes they feel needed to reduce cost and improve government efficiency. This resulted in a lot of federal workers losing their jobs. The United States government is America's largest employer, you would think that Trump and Musk would approach this task with extreme caution, but that was not the case. Musk's team of technocrats went rummaging through various government departments like a bull in a china shop.

Thus far, Trump and his DOGE team have hampered several federal departments by drastically cutting their budgets and purging tens of thousands of federal jobs, which is tantamount to the largest job cuts in U.S. history. According to a report published by CNBC.com, local economies like Washington, D.C., may suffer a recession.

Trump and Musk insist these budget cuts and massive job cuts are for the good of the nation. However, upon further examination of some of these changes, you'll find they benefit Elon Musk as well. Former U.S. Labor Secretary Robert Reich points out four departments that DOGE recommended firing workers that regulated Musk's businesses. They are the Food and Drug Administration, which regulates Neuralink; the Federal Aviation Administration, which oversees Space X; USAID, which probed Starlink; and the Consumer Financial Protection Bureau, which oversees Tesla's financing arm and a potential payment platform on X. These actions represent a blatant conflict of interest for Musk, yet few people outside of Reich have decried DOGE's actions.

According to reports, DOGE has access to millions of Americans' data. This includes their tax information, their social security information, and possibly their medical records if they're on Medicaid or Medicare. This is the ultimate overreach. It is an invasion of our privacy, and should not be tolerated under any circumstances.

As a man who made his money off technology, Musk, above all people, knows just how important and valuable having access to the data of millions of American citizens is. These DOGE technocrats answer to Musk, not the American people, and have carte blanche access to your personal data. There are no guarantees that this data won't be used nefariously against us or to benefit Musk in the future as he helps to create some sort of fascist dystopian society with whites at the top, Asians in the middle, and Blacks and Latinos at the bottom --the MAGA-inspired version of American Apartheid 2.0. To paraphrase the immortal words of the late great Gil Scott-Heron, "Why wait for [2026]? You can panic now and avoid the rush."

Apparently, I am not the only one who isn't feeling Trump's and Musk's recent actions, as a recent poll suggests. The majority of Americans are also uneasy with Musk and his technocratic minions' recent actions. The Washington Post's Aaron Blake writes that "there are increasing signs that the American people writ large don't have a ton of patience for a second billionaire — this one unelected — wielding such power over our politics." A recent AP-NORC poll found that Musk's popularity is decreasing. The poll shows that only 36% had a favorable opinion of him while 52% had an unfavorable opinion of Musk. According to Blake "Americans don't love the idea of the world's richest man throwing his weight around."

From an outside point of view, it appears that Musk wields an enormous amount of influence over Trump. It looks as though Musk is the real power behind the presidency and Donald Trump is nothing more than a well-paid figurehead who does nothing but embarrass himself at press conferences, sign executive orders, and take directions from Elon Musk.

Needless to say, this is not a good look for the millions of MAGA supporters who thought they were voting for Trump, an alpha male, who is his own man, not a beta male who takes directions from wimpy billionaires.

Well, I've got some bad news for MAGA supporters. When it comes to men who are richer than he is and more powerful than he is (can you say Vladimir Putin), Trump becomes a certified sycophantic beta male who is more loyal to his rich and powerful alpha male masters than he is to his own country.

References:

https://www.npr.org/2025/02/14/nx-s1-5298144/federal-layoffs-usda-hud-defense-trump
https://www.washingtonpost.com/politics/2025/02/20/trump-policies-opposed-by-americans/
https://news.gallup.com/poll/204050/trump-job-approval-points-below-average-one-month-mark.aspx

https://www.msnbc.com/top-stories/latest/trump-inflation-economy-biden-rcna192015
https://www.cnbc.com/2025/02/12/cpi-january-2025.html
https://finance.yahoo.com/news/gas-prices-are-headed-higher-and-a-ripple-effect-could-make-it-worse-in-certain-regions-164645500.html
https://www.pennlive.com/news/2025/02/donald-trumps-golfing-tab-in-first-month-of-second-term-you-wont-believe-how-much-he-spent.html
https://trumpgolftrack.com/
https://www.yahoo.com/news/donald-trump-already-spent-10-003317081.html
https://www.pennlive.com/news/2025/02/donald-trumps-golfing-tab-in-first-month-of-second-term-you-wont-believe-how-much-he-spent.html
https://www.cnbc.com/2025/02/23/how-trump-doge-job-cuts-may-affect-the-us-economy.html
https://www.washingtonpost.com/politics/2025/01/27/polls-show-views-souring-elon-musk-trumps-wingman/
https://fortune.com/2025/02/18/doge-fired-fda-employees-overseeing-elon-musk-neuralink/
https://www.cbsnews.com/news/consumer-financial-protection-bureau-under-trump-60-minutes/
https://x.com/RBReich/status/1893851121019478061

The Red Wave of Enslavement
Bob McNeil

Letter from the future
Edgar Manuel Cambaza

Dear Adam Smith,
It was all a myth.

Abe Abiding
Joseph B Pravda

I have another dream
Edgar Manuel Cambaza

I dreamed a dream where money spread its wings,
Bored of my hands, it sought another face;
It left me yearning, lost in empty space,
While silent sorrow bore a thousand stings.

Now I am but a cake bereft of cream,
Sweet money, love I never meant to skew,
Yet I am but one suitor in your queue,
And you race on, an engine fed by steam.

The tariffs rise and keep us worlds apart,
Yet still I dream that we shall meet again;
I linger in the shadows with my heart,

Waiting for the sun to dry this heavy rain.
Though now we fall, though broken be my art,
You'll find your way to heal our silent pain.

The woke shall be awaken
Edgar Manuel Cambaza

The woke shall be awakened
In the name of a brighter future,
For what we see is truly insane:
One must cancel the cancel culture.

How correct is "politically correct"?
How postmodern are our times now?
Whom are they trying to protect?
At what cost, and who reaps the vow?

The woke shall be awakened
From this endless illusion called freedom.
Perhaps the world shall be great again
If we pause and walk with a bit of wisdom.

We do not have to dance to the same song,
Just to fit and smile like a deepfake;
For we have the right to be wrong,
If wrong means truly to awake.

And if we are to be great again,
Yes—the woke shall be awakened.

The Mythological People of Color Coalition
*C Liegh McInnis**

The March 21, 2024, *Morning Newsletter* of the *New York Times* features an article, "Race and Politics," by **David Leonhardt** that discusses "the rightward shift among voters of color," particularly "Asians, Hispanics, and African Americans," and pinpoints that the "trend is pronounced among working-class voters [of color], defined as those without a four-year college degree. (The Democrats' performance among nonwhite voters with a college degree has held fairly stable.)" The full article can be read here. While class certainly plays a role in more people of color leaning right, there are a couple of more obvious reasons that have been mostly overlooked or ignored because, sometimes, the need to simplify and spin issues outweighs nuance. So, I'll start by saying that, as a Black Nationalist, I've never embraced the term "people of color" because I understand that African Americans were more on an island than most understood. Of course, I've used the term when it was applicable, but I always understood that African Americans have never had the latitude or convenience to hope that others join with us in our struggle. Thus, I've never had much faith in the Mythological People of Color Coalition. This is not to say that over the past sixty years many Asians, Hispanics/Latinos, and African Americans haven't had some success working collectively against white supremacy.

"In the late 1960s, for instance, Black and Asian activists led the **Third World Liberation Front Movement** to establish race and ethnic studies in college and university curriculums in California" (Demsas and Ramirez). But, often, those efforts have been hindered by "immigration and economic policies that have historically pitted these communities against one another" (Demsas and Ramirez). In reality, just because these three groups have been equally despised by white supremacists does not mean that they have been consistently aligned in their plans to obtain first-class citizenship in America.

First and foremost, the article treats Asians, Hispanics/Latinos, and African Americans like monoliths when we are discussing some of the most diverse people on the planet. Yet, even by white liberals, these groups are lumped together because many white people can only see them as flat, one-dimensional objects rather than the multidimensional humans that they are. When discussing Asian Americans, we are discussing at least six origin groups that include Chinese, Indian, Filipino, Vietnamese, Korean, and Japanese. These groups constitute "eighty-five percent of all Asian Americans," and this doesn't include "the other 15 Asian origin groups in this analysis [that] make up about two percent or less of the nation's Asian population." Moreover,

"The largest Asian origin groups in the U.S. differ significantly by income, education, and other characteristics. These differences highlight the wide diversity of the nation's Asian population and provide a counterpoint to the 'model minority' myth and the description of the population as monolithic. Highlighting these differences within the Asian population has been central to debates about how data about the group should be collected by governments, colleges and universities, and other organizations, and how it can be used to shape policies impacting the diverse U.S. Asian population" (Budiman and Ruiz).

This is similar to identifying Hispanics, which is why I added "Latino" even though Leonhardt only identifies Hispanics. When teaching world literature, I would often discuss the differences between those who identify as Hispanic, Latino (now Latinx), and Chicano.

"From September 15 to October 15, the US celebrates **Hispanic Heritage Month**, a formal recognition of the histories and cultures of Americans with ancestral ties to Spain, Mexico, the Caribbean, Central America, and South America... While celebrating this diverse array of cultures isn't limited to Hispanic Heritage Month alone, the month is bookended by the anniversaries of several Latin American countries' independence... While only the term 'Hispanic' is in the celebration's title, the observance honors an eclectic population. Latino, Latinx, Chicano, and other terms are used, sometimes interchangeably, yet they have distinct meanings...In the same way that 'Hispanic' identifies someone with Spanish roots, 'Chicano' refers to Americans of Mexican ancestry. These folks do not identify as Hispanic, which they feel would not account for their

Mexican mestizo (a mix of Spanish and Indigenous) heritage" (Carbonell-Ladish).

And, of course, when discussing African Americans, we must account for three elements. One, African Americans came from the largest continent with the most ethnic groups, speaking the most languages. Even the European colonizers/enslavers recognized this when grouping captured Africans to be disseminated across the world, making sure to put Africans from different tribes in groups to make it more difficult for them to communicate and plan an escape. Two, forced miscegenation, primarily through the rape of African women by white male slave owners, created even more nuance and separation in how people of African descent define themselves, which is all too often overly generalized into two groups of house slaves and field slaves as if these two groups had homogenous feelings and reactions to their enslavement. And, three, like the two other groups, the African-American response to their enslavement began with differing ideas of how best to become free and first-class citizens and has continued to be fragmented by income, education, geographic background, and other characteristics. All of this is to say that each of these groups barely agrees with their internal demographics. As such, it should not be surprising that Asians, Hispanics/Latinos, and African Americans have never been able to maintain an effective and long-lasting coalition against white supremacy. Yet, what cannot be ignored is that all three groups have often fallen victim to bickering between each other for the "perceived" one seat at the white man's table. This bickering is insanely myopic because only in America and Europe are people of color a minority; yet, these three groups have never been able to create a global or national coalition because, again, they have embraced a white supremacist notion/projection toward each other, especially as it relates to a prescribed hierarchy racial dominance. White people created the term "model minority," particularly for Asians, not necessarily to praise Asians but "to define African Americans as deficient and inferior to white people by using Asian Americans as a proxy or a pawn to serve that purpose" (Demsas and Ramirez), and these three groups have continued to haggle over the term rather than confront the group responsible for creating the term as a divide and conquer tactic.

 Despite being touted as the "model minority," Asians have faced a great deal of oppression in America. The "anti-Asian sentiment in the United States is not new — just look to the **Chinese Exclusion Act of 1882**, which banned Chinese immigrants from becoming US citizens, and **President Franklin Roosevelt**'s **executive order in 1942** that put Japanese Americans into internment camps" (Demsas and Ramirez). Yet, despite this reality, most (not all) Asians, socially and culturally, have never sought a long-term alliance with African Americans, opting to work in a more nationalist or cultural manner and vote Democratic only as it suited their particular aims. Dominating American and global capitalism has been their political agenda of choice, and their support of social programs/movements has only been in times when it lessened oppression or violence against them. Moreover, remember that it was Asian plaintiffs who filed the suit to end Affirmative Action and that China is one of the major current colonizers of Africa. (As a Black Nationalist, I never fought for Affirmative Action as I was more interested in working to have more African Americans embrace a movement of sovereignty rather than one of begging white folks to be nice to us. Yet, it is telling that Affirmative Action was ended by Asian plaintiffs.) Additionally, most people don't know that the Mississippi Delta has a history of a Chinese population that dates to the end of the Civil War when white "planters recruited the Chinese as a possible replacement for the freed African-American laborers" (Wilson). Yet, because many of these newcomers had a supportive Mother Country and could arrive with certain means, the Chinese soon "sought economic success rather than social recognition [and] turned to another activity — opening and running grocery stores...by the early 1870s" (Wilson). As a youth in Clarksdale, Mississippi, during the '70s and '80s, my neighborhood was bordered by a Chinese grocery store on one end and a Jewish grocery store on the other end with an always uneasy tension from the resentment of Afro-Mississippians who understood the complicated elements that allowed what they deemed as outsiders to be in a position to exploit them while taking advantage of the very rights that Afro-Mississippians had fought diligently to secure. To be clear, this is not to say that all Asians hate or look down on African Americans. The Chinese community has become a mainstay in the Mississippi Delta in various aspects of life. But, based on voting habits and economic conflicts, Asian Americans have never seen their liberation movement as inextricably tied to that of African Americans; thus, it's no surprise that more of them are leaning Republican.

Hispanics/Latinos are similar to African Americans because having their cultures deeply rooted in religion makes them traditionally conservative while being politically liberal only because of Jim Crow, segregation, and white supremacy in general. Like African Americans, most Hispanics/Latinos have been against gay marriage and abortion but tend to vote Democratic because of the Republican Party's racist policies. Yet, I've always been in the minority as one who perceived the Hispanic/Latino communities not as invested in their alliance with African Americans as we have been. My notion seems to be verified by research as "a majority of blacks (70%), but a smaller share of Hispanics (57%), say the groups get along very or fairly well" ("Do Blacks and Hispanics Get Along?"). Mostly, this has to do with many of them having a deeper connection to a Mother Country in ways that African Americans don't have with Africa, causing some of them to view African Americans in a lesser light. This manifests in Hispanics/Latinos having a more nationalistic approach to their citizenship as "Hispanics also are somewhat less enthusiastic than blacks about residential integration. Six-in-10 blacks compared with half of all Hispanics say they would like to see the country become more integrated in terms of minorities and whites living in the same neighborhoods"

("Do Blacks and Hispanics Get Along?"). Additionally, when one understands that colorism is as big of an issue in the Hispanic/Latino communities as it is within African-American communities, one realizes that, for them, to be black or African is to be lesser. This Hispanic/Latino self-hatred, manifested through colorism, was made clear to me by a former undergraduate student, **Reina Garcia**, when she wrote a paper for my world literature class, paralleling the issue of self-hatred explored in Sierra Leone writer **Adelaide Casely-Hayford's** short story, **"Mista Courifer,"** to the self-hatred in many Hispanic/Latino communities. "With all minority groups at risk of becoming vulnerable to white supremacy, there is one specific group that this story closely parallels. That is the Latino community in the U.S. Self-hatred among Latinos in America strongly manifests itself in stances on immigration, the validation of negative Latino stereotypes, and the effort to conform to European standards to fit in" (Garcia). Garcia's paper was so well-written that it was eventually published by literary icon **Ishmael Reed** in his publication *Konch Magazine*. Even though self-hated and colorism are both created by white supremacy, many Hispanics/Latinos continue to embrace and perpetuate the hierarchy of color as a way to win favor with and gain acceptance from the white power structure. However, the primary cause of growing tensions between Hispanics/Latinos and African Americans is the battle over economic gain. "In 1992, **Jack Miles** wrote a long essay about race in Los Angeles for the *Atlantic Monthly* magazine, **'Blacks vs. Browns.'** He was one of the first to describe competition for jobs, suggesting Hispanics were gaining the upper hand. 'America's older black poor and newer brown poor are on a collision course,' he wrote" (Buchanan). When one combines colorism and the competition for economic survival, it's not surprising that more Hispanics/Latinos are leaning Republican.

African Americans have been guilty of the same prejudice toward Asians and Hispanics, especially as increasingly more African Americans have embraced the anti-immigrant rhetoric. And, as mentioned above, African Americans have always been traditionally conservative. Yet, while 90 percent of them voted for Obama, many of them resented Obama's policies regarding gay rights and abortion. In short, increasingly more African Americans are starting to vote their faith rather than their civil rights agenda. (Of course, there is the issue of black self-hatred for which to account, which was proven by the **Doctors Kenneth and Mamie Clark Baby Doll Test** to be a major factor in how African Americans navigated life daily. "The Clarks concluded that 'prejudice, discrimination, and segregation' created a feeling of inferiority among African-American children and damaged their self-esteem," which often caused them to think and act negatively and destructively toward themselves and others ("A Revealing Experiment"). Therefore, when one combines self-hatred with general ignorance, you get a generation of gangbangers and **Sexyy Reds** riding for **Trump**.) More and more African Americans are being seduced from the pulpit to vote their faith over social justice issues. And, while that may seem problematic, some blame must be assigned to the Democrats who have seemingly overplayed the progressive agenda, not understanding the religious leanings of African Americans and Hispanics/Latinos. As some of y'all may recall, I wrote a commentary, "Keep Wokeness from *Purple Rain*," about the adaptation of *Purple Rain* into a Broadway play and the Gawd awful changes the young African-American playwright is making in the name of "progress" and the **Me Too Movement**. As such, I'm cool with gay rights and keeping abortion legal, but them woke muthafuckers must keep their hands off **Prince**. So, even I have a line.

Furthermore, Trump's tactics don't just appeal to the millions of white people who fear being replaced or suffering retribution for their past evils from the increasing population of colorful bodies. They also appeal to anyone who feels left out or omitted from what they see as a new "progressive" or "woke" power structure reshaping reality in a way that is foreign to them. In an email thread discussing Leonhardt's article, poet, editor, cultural critic, and literary theorist **Dr. Tony Bolden** explains that:

"African American writers, particularly the resistance tradition, is the best source of insight into the nature, and thus pertinent inclinations, of white supremacy as well as many Black folks' psychological reactions to their experiences. **Langston Hughes**' concern about this and other problems inspired him to create **Jesse B. Semple**. I think the best example, though, is **Richard Wright**'s 1940 essay, **"How Bigger Was Born,"** wherein he explains what is virtually the same phenomenon [Leonhardt] tries to explain, but Wright does so in ideological and political terms. And his foresight is such that if this trend actually exists, it proves Wright prescient...(By the way, **Frantz Fanon** also warned about this same (so-called?) problem.) But the current crop of thinkers are so passionate in their aversion to Black Literature, especially Black Arts writing, that they seem to have skipped right over it, and consequently find themselves scratching their heads in bemusement."

For an empirical backdrop, Bolden points us to two quotes from Wright's aforementioned essay:

"And I could hear Bigger Thomas standing on a street corner in America expressing his agonizing doubts and chronic suspicions, this: 'I ain't going to trust nobody. Everything is a racket and everybody is out to get what he can get for himself. Maybe if we had a true leader, we could do something.' And I'd know that I was still on the track of learning about Bigger"

"From these items, I drew my first political conclusions about Bigger: I felt that Bigger, an American product, a native son of this land, carried within him the potentialities of either Communism or Fascism. I don't mean to say that the Negro boy I depicted in *Native Son* is either a Communist or a Fascist. He is not either. But he is a product of a dislocated society; he is a dispossessed and disinherited man; he is all of this, and he lives amid the greatest possible plenty on earth and he is looking a feeling for a way out. Whether he'll follow some **gaudy, hysterical leader who'll promise rashly to fill the void in him**, or whether he'll come to an understanding with the millions of his kindred fellow workers under trade-union or revolutionary guidance depends upon the future drift of events in America. But, granting the emotional state, the tensity, the fear, the hate, the impatience, the sense of exclusion, the ache for violent action, the emotional and cultural under, **Bigger Thomas, conditioned as his organism is, will not become an ardent, or even a lukewarm supporter of the status quo.**"

As Bolden asserts, in these two quotes, Wright is clearer than Leonhardt because Wright, unlike Leonhardt, is not invested in and does not see the ultimate goodness of America as a concept or an execution of that concept. Furthermore, unlike Leonhardt, who wishes to minimize the reality or impact of white supremacy or Trump as merely a manifestation of white supremacy, Wright understands that two things can be true. Trump is the mouthpiece of white fear and rage that galvanizes millions of white people to support him, and, simultaneously, millions of people marginalized and oppressed by white supremacist policies can be attracted to a "gaudy, hysterical leader who'll promise rashly to fill the void in him" when they perceive that the political alternatives have failed them. As such, today's aforementioned "gangbangers and Sexyy Red" are the epitome or manifestation of Bigger "following some gaudy, hysterical leader who'll promise rashly to fill the void in [them]" because they believe that Trump gave them COVID checks.

Ultimately, anyone surprised at the growing number of Asians, Hispanics/Latinos, and African Americans voting for Trump hasn't thoroughly understood the tenuous relationships that have always existed between people of color. But, we (African Americans and Jews) have never had a real (transparent) discussion about that relationship either. Therefore, people of color are at a fork in the road. While I admire folks who understand the power of relationships and will work to maintain this collective, I've remained certain that African Americans have what we need to be a sovereign people if we can ever overcome the illness of self-hatred. As a Black Nationalist, this trend of more Asians, Hispanics/Latinos, and African Americans drifting right doesn't bother or surprise me nearly as much as it surprises most black integrationists. But, most black integrationists don't know the difference between integration and desegregation and don't know that black folks were initially fighting for desegregation rather than integration before their liberation movement was coopted by the American media, conservative and liberal whites, and some middle-class blacks, evidenced by white liberals forcing **John Lewis** to modify his **March on Washington** speech because many felt it was too radical and demanded too much. Very few alliances have provided long-term positives for African Americans mostly because African Americans have entered these relationships from a position of dependency, perpetuated by their self-hatred that hinders their sovereignty. Only when we take Fanon's advice to kill the oppressor dwelling within our minds will African Americans become whole beings capable of entering into relationships and alliances as equals able to negotiate the terms to our best interests. Until then, we'll remain like many of the countries of our Mother Continent, constantly being seduced into servitude by accepting aid that is actually a payday loan.

Bibliography

Block, Melissa and Elissa Nadworny. "The Legacy of the Mississippi Delta Chinese," *NPR.org*, March 18, 2017, https://www.npr.org/2017/03/18/519017287/the-legacy-of-the-mississippi-delta-chinese. Accessed March 25, 2024.

Bolden, Tony. "Re: The Morning: Race and politics." Received by Multiple Recipients. March 21, 2024. Email Correspondence.

Budiman, Abby and Neil G. Ruiz. "Key Facts about Asian Origin Groups in the US," *Pew Research Center.org*, April 29, 2021, https://www.pewresearch.org/short-reads/2021/04/ 29/key-facts-about-asian-origin-groups-in-the-u-s/. Accessed March 25, 2024.

Buchanan, Susy. "Tensions Mounting between Blacks and Latinos Nationwide," *Southern Poverty Law Center.org*, July 27, 2005, https://www.splcenter.org/fighting-hate/ intelligence-report/2005/tensions-mounting-between-blacks-and-latinos-nationwide. Accessed March 25, 2024.

Burnett, Patrick and Fironze Manji. *From the Slave Trade to "Free" Trade: How Trade*
   Undermines Democracy and Justice in Africa. Fahamu, 2007.

Carbonell-Ladish, Lorraine. "What's the Difference between Spanish, Hispanic, Chicano, Latin
American, and Latinx?," *Grammarly.com*, June 15, 2022, https://www.grammarly.com/ blog/latinx-vs-hispanic/. Accessed March 24, 2024.

Demsas, Jerusalem and Rachel Ramirez. "The History of Tensions—and solidarity—between
Black and Asian American Communities Explained," *Vox.com*, March 16, 2021. Accessed March 25, 2024.

"Debunking the Model Minority Myth," *Pacific Asian Museum.usc.edu*, https:// pacificasiamuseum.usc.edu/exhibitions/online-exhibitions/debunking-the-model-minority-myth/. March 25, 2024.

"Do Blacks and Hispanics Get Along?" *Pew Research Center.org*, January 31, 2008, https://www.pewresearch.org/social-trends/2008/01/31/do-blacks-and-hispanics-get-along/. Accessed March 25, 2024.

Garcia, Reina. "A Critical Analysis of Adelaide Casely-Hayford's 'Mista Courifer': Reflecting Identity Struggles in the Latino Community, *Konch Magazine*, March 2017, https://s3.us-east-2.amazonaws.com/konch-archives/a-critical-analysis-of-adelaide. Accessed March 25, 2024.

"Kenneth and Mamie Clark Doll," *National Park Service.org*, https://www.nps.gov/brvb/learn/historyculture/clarkdoll.htm. Accessed March 25, 2024.

Leonhardt, David. "Race and Politics," *The Morning Newsletter* of the *New York Times*, March 21, 2024, https://www.nytimes.com/2024/03/21/briefing/race-and-politics.html. Accessed March 21, 2024.

"A Revealing Experiment," *NAACP Legal Defense Fund.org*, 2024, https://www.naacpldf.org/brown-vs-board/significance-doll-test/. Accessed March 25, 2024.

Ruiz, Neil G. et al. "Asian Americans and the 'Model Minority' Stereotype," *Pew Research Center.org*, November 30, 2023, https://www.pewresearch.org/race-ethnicity/2023/11/30/asian-americans-and-the-model-minority-stereotype/. Accessed March 25, 2024.

Wilson, Charles. "Chinese in Mississippi: An Ethnic People in a Biracial Society," *Mississippi History Now.mdah.ms.gov*, November 2002, https://www.mshistorynow.mdah.ms.gov/ issue/mississippi-chinese-an-ethnic-people-in-a-biracial-society. Accessed March 25, 2024.

Wright, Richard. "How 'Bigger' Was Born: An Introduction." *Native Son. Archive.org*, https://archive.org/stream/in.ernet.dli.2015.499539/2015.499539.native-son_djvu.txt. Accessed March 21, 2024.

The Terror Called Trump
Bob McNeil

Look at Us
Isaac Kilibwa

S
i
n
g
l
e

f
i
l
e;

an illegal procession
home.

Healing
Isaac Kilibwa

Who knew that even strays wonder
at last into nostrils of a head
filled with night, into letters
shaped as a place?

Can we go back to the night
we met?

To pick once more at beryls
vandalised of gloss
by our fleeing, to remember love
laced with hunger

but to be wanted. All the same.
I am an old waste and a place of
desolation, every brick
of righteousness is dashed.

Heal me and I will be healed;
save me and I will be saved.

Ruins
Isaac Kilibwa

Godliness and contentment is great
gain yet

who truly has cared for their neighbour,
who in the empire has cared for Christ?

We love and it is the death of us to love,
we hate and it is pain then death. We fuss.

On a street a man is seen as a bridge
conducting pain, as a bouquet of self

preservation,
and blows into delocalized feelings.

It is enviable for a man to put his house
in order, for a son to grieve in embers long

after a country burnt. It is why we envy
and crucify christs, even false ones,

and run away from ruins we made after
devouring ourselves so, that the world calls it art.

Iniquity abounds and the love of many
sputters.

ManSwanSong
Joseph B Pravda

A Bell for Danny Martin
Tim Hall

Spring seemed to come early this year.
Crocuses bloomed,
daffodils peeked out,
tulips reached their arms toward the sun.
But Easter cut them down
with a cold blast of Winter.
And so did America
to the young life of Danny Gilbert.

Smiling, lively, well-liked,
nick-named "Opie,"
a car-nut – "grease monkey"
we used to call them –
worked at a refinery,
had a girl friend,
thought for himself,
had a Dad and a Mom who were rocks
against all evils,
Danny was a young flower
just blooming,
cut down
by street violence
in April,
the cruelest month.

Did he sell drugs?
No.
Did he abuse and corrupt women?
No.
Was he a gang-banger?
No.
He just tried
to live his life honestly,
but he was cut down.

Such a life
is not often praised
by the hypocritical press.
They write about famous men.
When such young people are killed
the press
sheds crocodile tears
but never points a finger at
the militarism of the rich.
Such young people are never encouraged
to rebel against the society that spawns such violence.
The hypocritical press
does not connect street violence
to the wars of Bush.
It blames rappers.
It does not connect street violence
to Bill Clinton
who empowered the cops and courts

to incarcerate a generation of Black men.
The hypocritical press does not blame
the obscenely greedy CEOs,
paid millions to fire honest workers,
it does not blame them.

It blames video games.

But it was them!

They shot him
a las once de la noche

alone in the street
at eleven o'clock at night

his life meant nothing to them
a las once de la noche

they were programmed to kill
at eleven o'clock at night

by the famous men
a las once de la noche

on the streets paved with crack
at eleven o'clock at night

brought by the famous men

a las once de la noche

it was turned into bullets
at eleven o'clock at night

and fired by their hands
a las once de la noche

los ratos ricos
the rich rodents

las cucarachas del imperialismo
the cockroaches of imperialism

y los perros del capitalismo
the dogs of capitalism

they killed him
a las once de la noche

they wanted to kill him in Iraq
they wanted to kill him in Iran
they wanted to kill him at Virginia Tech
but they killed him in Oakland
a las once de la noche

Uncle Sam wanted him
Condoleeza Rice wanted him
Dick Cheney wanted him

Carl Levin wanted him too

They wanted to kill him in Iraq
in Iran in Afghanistan in Somalia
in Chad in the Philippines

They must be disappointed
They killed him too soon

They killed him in Oakland
a las once de la noche

Let us now praise famous men

It is eleven o'clock
at night

-- April 14, 2007

To the Unknown Proletarian
Tim Hall

(a response to the IWW poem by an Unknown Proletarian)

Where is your headstone, scarred by wind and sleet,
That bears your modest, unassuming name?
Somewhere west of Fargo, high on the heaving plain
Where you, a Wobbly, struck, and would not reap the wheat?

Were you Gordon, miner, once, of Butte,
Scottish, class fighter, of labor-tautened stock,
Your lifeblood coined while crouching under rock,
Who struck against the leech who wears the suit?

Big wake you left upon the sea of grain;
Deep tunnel that you bored still gleams.
Your anonymity was never what it seems:
You live through verse and through the workers' gain.

Your hand, like millions, in death yet pries
That great class-lever, the proletarian rise.

"From Diplomacy to Innovation: The Changing Landscape of U.S.-Africa Relations"
Onward Mutapurwa

Introduction

The geopolitical landscape of Africa has long been a theater for global powers vying for influence, resources, and strategic partnerships. In recent decades, the competition between the United States and China has intensified, with Africa emerging as a critical battleground for this rivalry. Under Donald Trump's presidency, the U.S. adopted an "America First" approach that reshaped its foreign policy priorities, including its engagement with Africa. This essay explores whether the U.S., under Trump's leadership, will continue to assert its interests in Africa to counteract China's growing influence or shift its focus to other global arenas.

China's presence in Africa has been marked by ambitious infrastructure projects, such as the Belt and Road Initiative, and a non-interference policy that has resonated with many African nations (Ajibo 2021). These strategies have allowed China to establish itself as a dominant player in the region, often at the expense of liberal democratic values traditionally championed by the U.S. The decline of these values, coupled with China's economic and political investments, has created a complex dynamic that challenges America's ability to maintain its influence.

On the other hand, Trump's foreign policy has been characterized by a departure from traditional diplomatic norms. His administration's focus on domestic priorities, coupled with a reduction in foreign aid and diplomatic engagement, has raised questions about the U.S.'s commitment to Africa. The withdrawal of USAID funding, sanctions on African nations like South Africa, and its plan to close almost 8 embassies in Africa have signaled a shift in America's approach to the continent (The Africa report 2025). This shift reflects a broader strategy to prioritize technological innovation and green energy development, areas where the U.S. seeks to lead the global narrative.

The rise of climate change as a pressing global issue has further complicated the U.S.-China rivalry in Africa. As nations scramble to address environmental challenges, the demand for green technology and rare minerals has surged. Trump's administration has recognized the importance of these resources, as evidenced by its attempt to lure Kiev into a debt payment arrangement where it partners on an economic strategic partnerships to mine green minerals and other undiscoverable minerals as a way to secure Ukrainian security from Russia (CSIS 2025). This pivot toward technological hegemony suggests that the U.S. may prioritize innovation over traditional geopolitical influence in Africa.

In this context, the essay examines the implications of Trump's policies for U.S.-Africa relations and the broader geopolitical competition with China. It argues that while Africa remains a significant arena for global power struggles, the U.S. under Trump may choose to focus on future-oriented strategies that align with its technological and environmental goals. This shift could redefine the nature of U.S. engagement with Africa, moving away from traditional diplomacy and toward a more strategic and selective approach.

U.S. vs. China—The Battle for Hegemony in Africa

Africa has emerged as a pivotal arena in the global contest for influence between the United States and China. This competition is not merely about economic dominance but also about ideological and geopolitical supremacy. While the U.S. has historically positioned itself as a champion of liberal democracy and human rights (CRS Report 2025), China's approach has been markedly different, focusing on economic partnerships and a policy of non-interference. This section delves into the contrasting strategies of the two powers and their implications for Africa.

China's influence in Africa has grown exponentially over the past two decades, driven by its ambitious Belt and Road Initiative (BRI). This global infrastructure development strategy has seen China invest billions of dollars in African countries, building roads, railways, ports, and power plants (Council on foreign relations 2023). These projects have not only enhanced connectivity within the continent but also strengthened China's economic ties with African nations. For many African leaders, China's investments represent an opportunity to address critical infrastructure gaps without the stringent conditions often attached to Western aid. However, critics argue that these projects have led to a debt trap, where countries become heavily indebted to China, compromising their sovereignty.

In contrast, the U.S. has traditionally emphasized governance, transparency, and human rights in its engagement with Africa. Programs like the African Growth and Opportunity Act (AGOA) and the Millennium Challenge Corporation (MCC) have sought to promote trade and development while encouraging democratic reforms (Congressional research service 2023). However, these initiatives have often been overshadowed by China's more direct and tangible investments. The U.S.'s focus on democracy promotion has also been met with skepticism in some quarters, particularly in countries where authoritarian regimes have found a more accommodating partner in China.

One of the most significant points of divergence between the U.S. and China is their approach to military engagement in Africa. The U.S. has established a robust military presence on the continent through the United States Africa Command (AFRICOM) (Osifo 2022). This initiative aims to combat terrorism, promote regional stability, and protect U.S. interests. However, AFRICOM has been met with suspicion by some African nations, who view it as a tool for advancing American hegemony. In contrast, China's military engagement in Africa has been more limited, focusing primarily on peacekeeping missions under the United Nations. This restrained approach aligns with China's broader policy of non-interference, which has been well-received by many African leaders.

Trade is another area where the U.S. and China have adopted contrasting strategies. China's trade with Africa has grown significantly, surpassing that of the U.S. in recent years. Chinese companies have become major players in sectors such as mining, construction, and telecommunications. In contrast, U.S. trade with Africa has stagnated, with American companies often hesitant to invest in markets perceived as risky (Klomegar 2025). The U.S.'s reliance on sanctions and conditional aid has further strained its economic relationships with some African countries.

The ideological dimension of the U.S.-China rivalry in Africa cannot be overlooked. China's model of state-led capitalism and non-interference has gained traction in many African countries, particularly those with authoritarian regimes. This model offers an alternative to the liberal democratic values championed by the U.S., which some African leaders view as intrusive and paternalistic. The decline of liberal democracy in parts of Africa can be attributed, in part, to China's growing influence and its willingness to engage with regimes that the U.S. has sought to isolate (Hodzi 2022).

Despite these challenges, the U.S. retains significant advantages in its engagement with Africa. American universities, cultural institutions, and non-governmental organizations have established deep ties with African communities. The U.S. also remains a major provider of humanitarian aid and development assistance, addressing critical issues such as health, education, and food security. However, these efforts have often been undermined by inconsistent policies and a lack of strategic focus like withdrawal of USAID funding.

In conclusion, the U.S.-China rivalry in Africa reflects a broader struggle for global influence. While China's economic investments and non-interference policy have resonated with many African nations, the U.S.'s emphasis on governance and human rights continues to hold appeal in certain quarters. The challenge for the U.S. is to adapt its strategies to remain competitive in a rapidly changing geopolitical landscape. This requires a nuanced understanding of Africa's diverse needs and aspirations, as well as a willingness to engage with the continent on its own terms.

Trump's Foreign Policy—America First and Its Consequences

The presidency of Donald Trump ushered in a fundamental shift in American foreign policy, characterized by an emphasis on nationalism and an "America First" agenda (European student think tank 2025). This approach prioritized domestic economic interests and national security over traditional diplomatic engagements, leading to significant consequences for U.S.-Africa relations. Unlike previous administrations that actively sought to expand American influence on the continent through trade agreements, developmental aid, and diplomatic initiatives, Trump's administration deprioritized Africa, focusing instead on economic competition with China, technological advancement, and military strategy. The impact of this shift was most visible in the U.S.'s reduced political engagement with African nations, its withdrawal of key developmental programs, and its increasing reliance on economic leverage rather than diplomatic outreach.

Trump's Isolationist Approach to Africa

While previous American presidents sought to build alliances with African nations through development assistance and multilateral cooperation, Trump's administration embraced a more isolationist stance, reducing foreign aid and diplomatic missions on the continent. Under the America First doctrine, Trump frequently questioned the benefits of engaging with Africa, arguing that U.S. resources should be spent on domestic priorities rather than overseas assistance (Ogunbukola 2024). This sentiment resulted in several key policy changes that weakened diplomatic ties between Washington and African capitals.

One of the most notable changes was the significant reduction in USAID funding for African development projects. USAID has historically been a cornerstone of U.S. foreign policy in Africa, providing economic support, healthcare initiatives, and infrastructure development to struggling nations. However, Trump's administration significantly cut funding for African programs (Imray 2025), leaving many nations searching for alternative partners—primarily China, which readily filled the void with investment.

Additionally, Trump threatened to withdraw U.S. embassies from certain African nations, citing cost-cutting measures and a lack of strategic necessity. Diplomacy and cultural exchange programs were affected, diminishing America's soft power influence on the continent. Many African leaders viewed these moves as a signal that Washington was disengaging, further opening the door for China and other rising global players to increase their footprint.

Sanctions and U.S. Relations with African Leadership

Trump's administration also took a firm stance on governance and human rights violations, imposing sanctions on African leaders and governments accused of corruption or authoritarian practices. While the intention was to uphold democratic values, many African nations perceived these actions as hypocritical and an attempt to engineer regime change (Herald 2016), particularly given the U.S.'s own political challenges and controversial foreign interventions in the past.

Sanctions against leaders such as Zimbabwe's Emmerson Mnangagwa and South Africa's Jacob Zuma reinforced the belief among African nations that Washington's interest was not in genuine partnership but in punitive measures. These actions further strengthened China's influence, as Beijing's foreign policy of non-interference (Council of Foreign relations 2022) made it an attractive alternative. African leaders who felt targeted by U.S. sanctions began leaning more heavily on China, which offered investment and diplomatic engagement without imposing political conditions.

China's stance contrasted starkly with the U.S., particularly in institutions like the United Nations, where Washington often advocated for accountability and intervention, while Beijing vetoed resolutions that sought to impose penalties on African governments. The result was a growing divide between African leadership and U.S. policymakers, reinforcing perceptions that China was a more reliable ally in regional governance issues.

The Suspicion Surrounding AFRICOM and U.S. Military Presence in Africa

While the U.S. has maintained a strong military presence in Africa through AFRICOM (United States Africa Command), Trump's administration did not actively expand military operations in the region, instead shifting attention to countering China's military buildup in the Pacific and responding to threats in the Middle East.

AFRICOM was met with skepticism from many African governments, who viewed it as a form of military intervention rather than genuine security cooperation. Unlike China, which has avoided direct military involvement in Africa aside from participating in peacekeeping missions, the U.S. maintained a network of bases across the continent, conducting operations against extremist groups like Boko Haram and Al-Shabaab (Country reports on terrorism 2019). While these operations were ostensibly aimed at protecting African nations from terrorist threats, some leaders believed they were an extension of U.S. geopolitical interests rather than a sincere attempt to stabilize the region.

China's alternative approach military aid without active intervention proved more palatable to African governments, further eroding the perception of American involvement as beneficial. In contrast to the U.S., China's strategic focus relied more on economic expansion and political alliances rather than military engagement, solidifying its foothold in Africa without provoking widespread suspicion.

Trade and Economic Relations: U.S. vs. China in Africa

One of the most defining aspects of U.S.-Africa relations during Trump's presidency was the declining trade ties between Washington and African nations. Historically, trade agreements such as AGOA (African Growth and Opportunity Act) had helped boost U.S.-Africa economic relations, facilitating duty-free exports from Africa to the U.S. While AGOA remained in place, Trump's administration failed to significantly expand American trade with Africa especially his increment of trade tarrifs between USA and Africa reflect how Africa is not the focal point (Oyedijo and Akenroye 2025), allowing China to further dominate the continent's economic landscape.

China's Belt and Road Initiative (BRI) provided African countries with substantial economic opportunities (Kuiver 2024), including direct loans for infrastructure projects. In contrast, U.S. trade policies under Trump relied on the Washington Consensus, a set of market-driven principles that emphasized privatization and economic liberalization. However, many African nations viewed the Washington Consensus as less favorable compared to China's direct financial aid model, leading them to strengthen trade partnerships with Beijing instead.

China's aggressive infrastructure development including highways, ports, and railways made Beijing's economic engagement more appealing. U.S. corporations struggled to compete with China's state-backed enterprises, which could offer large-scale investment with fewer conditions. Trump's administration did not present an alternative economic model that could rival China's influence, ultimately allowing Beijing to consolidate its role as Africa's leading economic partner.

Conclusion: The Shift Away from Africa

Trump's foreign policy choices reflected a fundamental shift in America's global priorities, moving away from traditional geopolitical influence in Africa and toward economic and technological competition with China. The reduction in diplomatic efforts, sanctions on African leaders, and withdrawal of developmental assistance all signaled a disinterest in maintaining strong relations with African nations.

At the same time, Trump's focus on AI, green technology, and economic restructuring indicated that America's primary concern was future innovation rather than expanding influence through conventional geopolitical means. This transition marked the emergence of a new global narrative centered on technological supremacy rather than territorial or political dominance, reinforcing the idea that Washington viewed Africa as secondary to broader global ambitions.

China, on the other hand, capitalized on America's disengagement, further solidifying its role as Africa's key economic and political partner. The non-interference policy, large-scale infrastructure investments, and a hands-off approach to governance made Beijing the preferred partner for many African nations. As the world moves toward a technology-driven future, the next phase of global influence will be determined by nations that lead in artificial intelligence, green energy, and sustainable innovation areas in which Trump positioned the U.S. as a frontrunner, albeit at the expense of traditional African engagement.

The Shift from Geopolitics to Technological Hegemony

The global landscape is undergoing a profound transformation, driven by the urgent need to address climate change and the rapid advancement of technology. Under Donald Trump's presidency, the United States began to pivot away from traditional geopolitical strategies, focusing instead on technological innovation and green energy as the cornerstones of its global influence. This shift has significant implications for U.S.-Africa relations, as the continent's role in supplying critical resources for green technology becomes increasingly important. In this section, we explore how the U.S. is redefining its approach to global hegemony, moving from geopolitics to technology-driven leadership, and what this means for Africa.

Climate Change and the Rise of Green Technology

Climate change has emerged as one of the most pressing challenges of the 21st century (Abass et al 2022), reshaping global priorities and driving the demand for sustainable solutions. The transition to green technology—such as renewable energy, electric vehicles, and carbon capture systems—has become a focal point for nations seeking to lead the fight against climate change. For the U.S., this represents an opportunity to assert its dominance in a new era of technological hegemony.

Under Trump's administration, the U.S. made significant investments in green technology, recognizing its potential to drive economic growth and secure global leadership. This shift was evident in Trump's deal with Ukraine, which prioritized access to green minerals like lithium as part of the payment for U.S. support. Lithium and other rare earth elements are essential for the production of batteries, solar panels, and other green technologies, making them critical resources in the race to combat climate change.

Africa, with its abundant reserves of green minerals, has become a key player in this transition. Countries like the Democratic Republic of Congo, Zimbabwe, and South Africa possess vast deposits of lithium, cobalt, and other rare earth elements, positioning them as strategic partners in the global green revolution. However, the U.S.'s focus on securing these resources has raised questions about its commitment to broader engagement with Africa, as the continent's role is increasingly defined by its resource potential rather than its geopolitical significance.

Artificial Intelligence and Technological Innovation

In addition to green technology, artificial intelligence (AI) has emerged as a critical area of competition in the quest for global leadership (GIS reports 2025). AI has the potential to revolutionize industries, enhance national security, and address complex challenges such as climate change and healthcare. Under Trump's presidency, the U.S. prioritized AI development, increasing funding for research and fostering partnerships with tech giants like Elon Musk's Tesla and Jeff Bezos's Amazon.

The emphasis on AI reflects a broader strategy to position the U.S. as a leader in technological innovation, moving away from traditional geopolitical influence. This shift has implications for Africa, as the continent's technological infrastructure remains underdeveloped compared to other regions. While China has invested heavily in building Africa's digital infrastructure, the U.S. has focused on advancing its own technological capabilities, leaving African nations to rely on Chinese support for their digital transformation.

The U.S.'s pivot to AI and green technology highlights a fundamental change in its approach to global hegemony. Rather than competing with China through traditional means, such as military presence and trade agreements, the U.S. is seeking to redefine the narrative by leading the technological revolution. This strategy aligns with Trump's America First mantra, prioritizing domestic innovation and economic growth over international engagement.

Africa's Role in the New Global Order

As the U.S. shifts its focus to technology-driven leadership, Africa's role in the global order is evolving. The continent's vast reserves of green minerals and its growing population make it a critical player in the transition to a sustainable future. However, the U.S.'s approach to Africa under Trump has been marked by a lack of strategic engagement, raising concerns about the long-term implications of this shift.

China, in contrast, has continued to strengthen its ties with Africa, investing in infrastructure, trade, and technology (Munyati 2024). The Belt and Road Initiative has expanded China's influence across the continent, providing African nations with the resources and support needed to develop their economies. This has positioned China as a more reliable partner for Africa, particularly as the U.S. focuses on its own technological ambitions.

The U.S.'s disengagement from Africa under Trump reflects a broader trend in its foreign policy, prioritizing future-oriented strategies over traditional alliances. While this approach may yield benefits in terms of technological innovation and economic growth, it risks alienating African nations and ceding influence to China. As the world moves toward a new era of technological hegemony, the U.S. must consider how to balance its domestic priorities with its international responsibilities.

Conclusion: The Future of U.S.-Africa Relations

The shift from geopolitics to technological hegemony represents a significant change in the U.S.'s approach to global leadership. Under Donald Trump, the U.S. has prioritized green technology and artificial intelligence as the cornerstones of its strategy, moving away from traditional engagement with Africa. While this approach aligns with America's long-term goals, it raises questions about the future of U.S.-Africa relations and the continent's role in the new global order.

Africa's abundant resources and strategic importance make it a key player in the transition to a sustainable future. However, the U.S.'s focus on technological innovation has led to a reduction in diplomatic and economic engagement with African nations, creating opportunities for China to expand its influence. As the world enters a new era of technological competition, the U.S. must consider how to balance its pursuit of innovation with its commitment to global partnerships.

Ultimately, the future of U.S.-Africa relations will depend on the ability of both nations to navigate this evolving landscape. For Africa, the challenge lies in leveraging its resources and strategic importance to secure meaningful partnerships that support its development goals. For the U.S., the challenge lies in balancing its technological ambitions with its responsibility to engage with the global community. As the world moves toward a new era of technological hegemony, the U.S. and Africa must find ways to work together to address the challenges and opportunities of the 21st century.

Conclusion: The Future of U.S.-Africa Relations in an Era of Technological Hegemony

The geopolitical dynamics between the United States and China in Africa have historically been shaped by competing ideologies, trade agreements, and strategic partnerships. However, under Donald Trump, the U.S. began shifting in Africa, favoring a future-oriented strategy centered on technological supremacy. This transition reflects America's evolving priorities moving from military influence and diplomatic relations to leadership in artificial intelligence, green technology, and the global climate transition.

While China continues to expand its foothold in Africa through direct infrastructure investments, debt diplomacy, and trade agreements, the U.S.'s disengagement from Africa suggests a strategic calculation: rather than competing with China on the same geopolitical terms, Washington appears focused on leading the next wave of global innovation. This pivot toward artificial intelligence, renewable energy, and green minerals indicates a broader redefinition of hegemony, where influence is derived from controlling technological and environmental narratives rather than securing physical territories or regional alliances.

Africa, with its abundant reserves of lithium, cobalt, and other rare-earth elements essential for green technology, remains a critical player in this emerging landscape. However, Trump's approach deprioritized diplomatic and economic engagement with Africa, making China the dominant partner for many nations seeking investment and stability. As a result, African governments must carefully assess the long-term implications of deepening reliance on Beijing while navigating a world increasingly driven by technological power rather than traditional geopolitical dominance.

Ultimately, the U.S. under Trump did not prioritize strengthening African relations as a tool to counter China's influence. Instead, it focused on securing technological leadership, positioning itself at the forefront of artificial intelligence and green energy. This marks the beginning of a new phase in global power dynamics—one where hegemony is no longer determined solely by territorial control but by technological advancement and environmental leadership. Africa now faces a critical crossroads: whether to align itself primarily with China's state-backed economic model or engage strategically with the U.S.'s emerging technological dominance to shape its own future.

As the global order transforms, Africa's ability to leverage its resources and partnerships will determine its position in the next era of global influence. The continent must recognize that the battle for hegemony is no longer defined by political ideology alone but by who controls the future of technological innovation and sustainability. In this regard, Africa's choices today will shape its geopolitical and economic trajectory for decades to come.

Reference List

Abbass. K, Qasim. M. Z, Song. H, Murshed. M, Mahmood. H and Younis. I. (2022). A review of the global climate change impacts, adaptation, and sustainable mitigation measures. Environ Sci Pollut Res 29, 42539–42559 (2022). https://doi.org/10.1007/s11356-022-19718-6

Ajibo. C. (2021). Belt and Road initiative meets Africa: Exploring the state of play, the implications and the imperative for complementarities of interests Article in Journal of Comparative Law in Africa · DOI: 10.47348/JCLA/v8/i2a1

Country Reports on Terrorism (2019), Bureau Of Counterterrorism.

Congressional Research Service. (2025). Democracy and Human Rights in U.S. Foreign Policy: Evolution, Tools, and Considerations for Congress. https://crsreports.congress.gov

European Student ThinkTank. America First 2.0 - The New Trump Administration And The Next Four Years. Special Issue. Vol. 1, NO. 1, 1-63

Hodzi, O. (2022). The China Effect: Democracy and Development in the 21st Century. Asia Policy, 17(3), 51-60. https://www.jstor.org/stable/27227217

Imray. G. (2025). Trump's permanent USAID cuts slam humanitarian programs worldwide: 'We are being pushed off a cliff'. The Associated Press.

Lenderts, C.S., (2014). "Security Threats in Perspective: Understanding the Failures of American Foreign Policy in Africa". CMC Senior Theses. Paper 929. http://scholarship.claremont.edu/cmc_theses/929

Munyati. C. (2024). Why strong regional value chains will be vital to the next chapter of China and Africa's economic relationship. World Economic Forum. CNBC Africa. https://www.cnbcafrica.com/2024/why-strong-regional-value-chains-will-be-vital-to-the-next-chapter-of-china-and-africas-economic-relationship/

Ogunbukola. M. (2019). Implications of Trump's Foreign Policy on Africa, the Middle East, and Global Power Dynamics

Osifo, A, (2022). "USAFRICOM: An Analysis of the United States Africa Command and the Forces that Legitimize and Justify US Military Presence in Africa". Scripps Senior Theses. 1855. https://scholarship.claremont.edu/scripps_theses/1855

Scheneider. H. (2025). Who is at the fore front of AI Innovation.
https://www.gisreportsonline.com/c/technology/

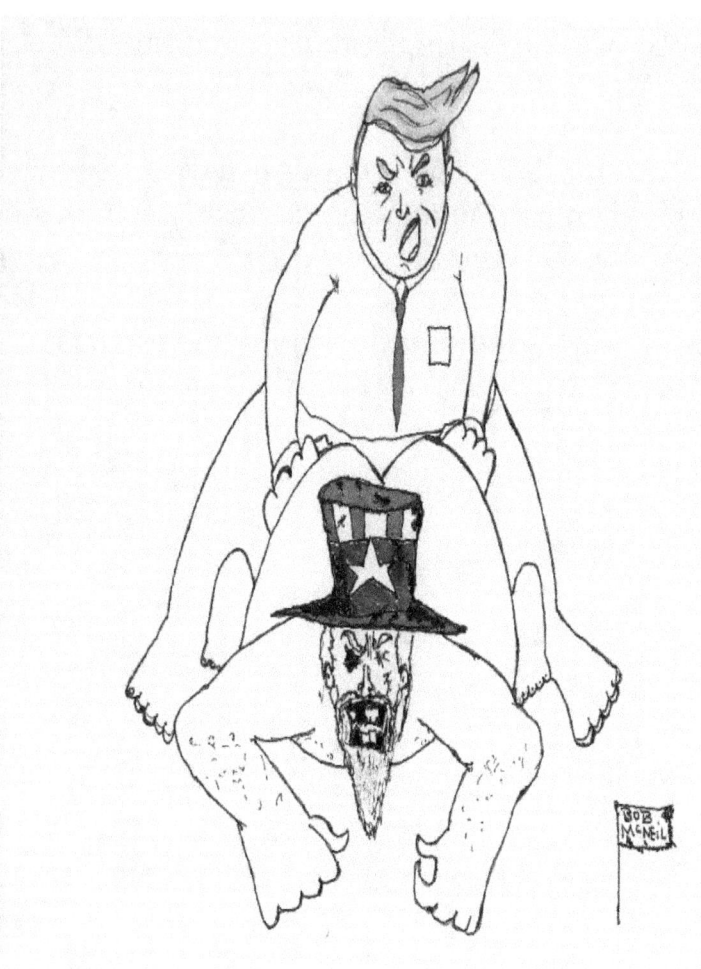

Trump humping Sam
Bob McNeil

Curated Selections from myactivity.google.com
Tiffany L. Hendrix

Week 1: Maybe Europe Will Save Us.

Searched for *quotes about hope*
Searched for *ICE raids Chicago*
Watched *YaniSs Odua & FNX One Love [Clip Officiel]*
Searched for *where were there deportations today*
Watched *Chicago Mayor Johnson dodges questions on migrant funding*
Searched for *fix your heart or die reference*
Searched for *how do I find out what my google voice number is*
Viewed *Smashit Break Room*
Searched for *what companies are keeping dei*
Searched for *[redacted] county public library*
Visited *countdown to january 20 2029*

Week 2: Maybe China Will Save Us.

Searched for:
how to report someone using pronouns in Colorado
what is the gayest thing i can watch on netflix right now
how many days has it been since trump has been president this time
plans for surviving inflation
will i still have access to my audible books after canceling
elon musk access to treasury

how does ICE even know if someone is undocumented
a day without immigrants protest

Week 3: Nobody Will Save Us. We Have To Save Ourselves.

Searched for:
red cards
god ain't petty but i am
intent vs. impact
Watched *YaniSs Odua & FNX One Love [Clip Officiel]*
Searched for *human rights campaign*
feb 28 economic blackout
what to do with my stuff if i leave the country

From ramblings of A House Wife.
Bahiirwa Catherine

My husband spent quite a number of hours glued on the screen: TV and phone during the USA campaigns and elections last year. He loves podcasts, from Joe Burden to Owen Caddace. So, he literary listens to a lot especially if it has a word American on it. One day he used my instagram and followed quite a number of pages that I unfollowed after realizing their American lives had nothing to do with me, a Ugandan house wife. On the day trump was officially announced the president elect, I had called to ask for something, you know house wif- ish with the two toddlers. He said, "Trump has won! Do you believe it?" I said, "Yeah I knew it."

"How? When Kamala had all the celebrity endorsements." I said yeah and giggled at the end. And while I posed, the conversation moved to something else. You know domestic.

But I wanted to tell him that the democrats forgot that they had used celebrity endorsements with Biden and it wouldn't work with Kamala or that the Obamas used race during their term and it couldn't work for Kamala right after Biden. And that Trump this time had appealed to the emotional senses of the public, he had not cared for the corporates. So they voted him. Even the blacks. But what would a housewife who spends half the time when kids are asleep lip-syncing on tiktok, he wouldn't listen to me. The same way my work colleagues did not during every Israel and Palestine debate during breaks because I was that corner employee with a book in her face, they thought I was reading a romantics and they forgot I read Mahmoud Darwish. Maybe because I loved how he wrote his pain on paper or how his name sounded exotic.

But like I usually say, from my social point of view, did I also forget to tell you that half my rich friends became jobless days after they had spent so much as per the Ugandan youth standard on my birthday gifts because they already know I am shy and parties would not cut it for me?. And I don't want you to forget that my friends group is millennial. Did I mention that my birthday is 20th of January? So I believe I know first-hand or maybe second hand what Trump's second coming means to the rest of the world, and of course from my social point of view...

I really don't blame the president of the United States to have China as a dominant word in his vocabulary nowadays. Being in competition with a country that fought colonialists with martial arts is definitely a scare, imagine being a CEO with a bachelors in economics yet in competition with an underdog CEO, its scary right. Because your loss is inevitable. Why? It can be like it is your time to face what they faced , but on your down side is that your body and mind isn't built for such hard work, so you resort to your privileged tactics i.e. tantrums, blackmail and gang kidnaps. Well, where I come from they say "asabade lya bumba" which directly translates to "he has sailed on a clay boat" apparently his domestic and foreign policies might go on war, stopping China imports to the US is something to laugh about just as many African exports to the USA come cheaply for guilt and terms of foreign aid, however, when that is scrapped, I hope I live to see when African exports to the west actually get what they are worth.

When I listen to president Trump I get dejavu of when the Ugandan president and the Rwandese president were on war. Apparently, from 2019 to 2023 the Rwanda-Uganda boarder was locked. Rwandese or as per the Ugandan constitution, Banyarwanda, constitute a more than 30% total of the population where a 40% of each tribal group has inter married with their women , making the total magnitude of Rwandese influence more than we as Ugandans want to admit. So the reason for closure despite what was told the public, it was allegedly a lost gold truck to Rwanda from the DRC through Uganda. Our presidents are figuratively brothers. So it was a sibling rivalry that punished a population worth mentioning. It makes sense to believe that what Trump has on China is just a business rivalry for he is a business man first then the president of the United States of America.

Most of us "social critics" actually look at the USA right now as a contemporary African polygamist man. Why use contemporary is that he has one wife, un numbered women and un numbered children. But tries to be a husband and father to all of them at the early stages of their lives, both spouse relationship and life of the children. However, in the later stages when he feels burdened, starts to complain, puts curfews, and diminishes the home budgets and when the women start to raise their grievances he cuts off one by one till he becomes a deadbeat father. However, none of them called him to sire with them and none of the off springs of course applied to be his. In the same binding, the USA birthed all these organisations. The African civilization, truth be told is suffering fixations till we grow at a naturally designated pace. I want to believe the founders of US AID wanted to give back what they had taken, minerals and labour from Africa, oil and labour from Asia. Ha-ha! From my africanacity point of view the USA owes us the AID

From the outside really it's hard to say who is American, because everyone in the world is American. This is where **PRESIDENT** Trump becomes confused too. His idea of what, who, where, when , how is America or American might come from his Caucasian biases no wonder that was what the democrats put on the fore front much as of course their agendas and the world order didn't sit well with humanity especially from the social point of view. I want to believe what he wants for "the Americans" is really what he wants for the Americans. He calls them immigrants yet they call themselves Americans. It's like watching South African idols or any other reality South African TV show and if not schooled that Boers are Afrikaans, you get a culture shock, or hearing a white say they are zims or Kenyans. It happens all the time. What Trump did in his first coming was like if Mandela had told the whites to pack in 1994. Funnily, in his second coming, he is like a father of many requiring a paternity test every time he is to dish out food, shelter, medicine and school fees. He should maybe learn a few lessons from the Ugandan president where he has led a country with a magnitude of unrelated ethnic groups for over 30 years. No wonder president Putin has got a liking to him.

That brings us to the fact that the world became a global village really. When you come to Africa we leave a village chief to live through his leadership. Whereby a chief is selected in the prime of his age, marries, gets children and grandchildren, then every family wants their daughter to marry the chief's off springs whereas the traditional families wouldn't want their children to get entangled with the chief's contaminated family. This was because every contamination started with chief's family. They got formal education first and the rest is written in history books. The chief however, on his death bed usually from old age, though might want one of his children to be his predecessor, it rarely happened. So another chief was selected based on his accomplishments in his youthfulness. I want to remind you that we live in a global village. Before USA we had Britain both unique of each other so, what do we say if we are now transcending to China. We are in a village after all. And every university where I come from has a Confucius school, teaching Chinese at a small cost. They started to build water taps where USA had boreholes in our slums. I am just waiting to take on my Chinese classes when it becomes free of charge. However, I don't know how it will work when Islam is becoming what china is becoming yet they have no intersection. At least Christianity and the west had an intersection.

On this day still, we want to thank god for social media especially tiktok, YouTube and twitter. But mainly tiktok and the brave soldiers of truth. Why call them brave. They show their faces alongside the truth. *Tekikolebwa mutitizi.* So we leant that the economy champion has the biggest number of homeless people and homeless shelters, half the population living life on credit, a population I cannot imagine cannot have health care without cash or an insurance, and their state schools care about enrollment but not the output. And yet funny enough, the education curriculum that put them in this predicament is what the Ugandan education ministry adopted in 2021. {That will be for another day} aid to other countries ought to have come from the country's surplus capital. And he believes he as an individual can take his country from 3 to 6. Which might be right? But he cannot be on the two sides of the coin i.e. a business man with business associates apparently he has put on the fore front of bettering their economy and a president who wants to elevate his people's economic status. What will come of the capitalist when everyone lives better? What I am trying to say is that he should not blame other countries for what is happening in his country. He is creating a circus. It is only a tease. Eventually nothing will really happen with the python or the lion, but rather we will go back to our beds in our homes. Of course as the world we watch and pray he doesn't cause an unnecessary war like one of Ukraine and Russia where if only Biden hadn't come after his circus teases he wouldn't have had anything to prove.

At the end of the day we are just humans, pawns on a chess board moved by individuals, who are in turn on their own chess board, and the cycle will never end as long as we still have different theories to how humanity came to be. It reminds me of the four spheres in life {I lack a better term to use} i.e. Religion, social relations, finances and political involvement in that order but no human will ever attain them all in that order yet few humans are capable of living off order and President Trump isn't one of them. So at the end of the order he looked back and hates that he has followed an order. What he is doing is throwing a tantrum because there has been a lot of things he thought that he was doing right on his own accord and then he realizes that he is just a pawn like the people he looked down on and called pawns. I believe China might or might not be the next thing. We cannot deny how vast their influence has stretched on Africa and the world over, from processed food to the tiniest things like razor blades and needles. Give it to our dictator presidents to rush in welcoming Chinese communism, which we all know is pseudo, after the west closing aid doors.

How small feeble things kill big men, wish we could ask David or Helen of troy.

Shadows of Democracy
Mthokozisi Ncube

In twilight's hush, where shadows play
Democracy's fate is weighed
A leader rises, bold and bright
But at what cost, and with what might?

His words are laced with venom and spite
As institutions tremble, and norms take flight
The people watch, with hearts aflame
As democracy's fabric is torn and frayed

Yet still we hope, that from the ashes cold
A phoenix rises, young and bold
To reclaim the values, that once shone bright
And guide us forward, through the dark of night.

The Trump Effect
Mthokozisi Ncube

A stormy sea, with waves crashing high
The Trump effect, that reaches far and wide
From Africa's shores, to North America's gate
A ripple effect, that alters the global state

Sanctions and tariffs, a game of might
As economies tremble, and trade takes flight
The strong get stronger, the weak get worn
As the USA flexes, its muscles torn

Yet in the chaos, a chance is born
For new alliances, and a new dawn
Where cooperation, and mutual respect entwine
And the world finds peace, in a new rhyme.

Beyond the Phenomenon
Mthokozisi Ncube

A phenomenon, that captivates and repels
A leader, who defies, and compels
But beyond the noise, and the Twitter storm
Lies a world, that's weary, and forlorn

The climate cries, the poor lament
As diseases spread, and hope is spent
The world looks on, with a mixture of shame
And a longing for leaders, with a different aim

Yet still we rise, with a glimmer of hope
A chance to rebuild, and a new scope
To create a world, that's just and fair
Where love and kindness, are the values we share.

"This or That?": Voting for Vice President Kamala Harris Despite Democratic Debacle and Cowardice
C Liegh McInnis

Like most black people, I usually vote for the lesser of two evils. As I wrote years ago in my poem, **"Mississippi Like...,"** "When you vote, even though there are two flap-jack/ politicians on both sides of the ballot, and the concept of/ Statesman is nothing more than a mascot for Delta State,/ yet you pull the lever anyway because Medgar's blood/ is the only registration card you need,/ that's the Mississippi in ya'" (here). Rarely in national elections and probably only half the time in local elections are black people casting votes for a candidate that they think actually has their best interest at heart. Moreover, as a Black Nationalist, I only vote as a stopgap while I work to get more black folks to understand that constantly begging your oppressor to be nice to you is not a liberation plan. For more transparency, my pops went from being a civil rights street soldier who was arrested on multiple occasions while fighting for liberation to being the **Executive Vice Chair of the Mississippi Democratic Party**. (Y'all can read more of his accomplishments here.) As such, I know exactly how the machine works. And, one of the major issues or limitations of the Democrat Party is that it is still filled with a sizable amount of white members who feel as though they are constantly straddling the fence between appeasing black folks while working to ingratiate themselves to enough conservative whites to win an election. The problem is that the term, "appeasing," does not mean that they agree with or plan to implement a full plan of action designed to deconstruct systematic oppression. They merely need black folks to "feel" like progress is happening or that, again, Democrats are the best of the bad choices. As bleak as this may seem, **Vice President Kamala Harris** is the only alternative to the neo-Confederates reclaiming America and implementing **Project 2025**, which is merely a reboot of the Republican Party's 1994 **Contract with America** aka **Contract on Black America** bridged to the present by the 2009 **Tea Party Movement**. In short, the history of black voting can be summarized by **Black Sheep**'s anthem, **"The Choice Is Yours,"** in which they declare, "You can get with this, or you can get with that/ I think you'll get with this, for this is kinda phat" (here). Yet, most times, for black folks, the choice isn't phat, but we've remained discerning enough to be utilitarian in our choices when utopia wasn't available. Or, as any good **Spades** player knows, sometimes you just gotta go board to get some stay-here to keep from getting a wheel or a Boston run on ya!

This reality, by the way, doesn't make black folks stupid or hapless. Most black folks have known this since we switched from **President Abraham Lincoln**'s Republican Party the moment that the **1964 Democratic National Convention**—crashed by the **Mississippi Freedom Democratic Party** with the eloquence of civil rights legend **Fannie Lou Hamer**—sent the **Dixie-crats** running like rats and roaches into the Republican Party. This transition was cemented sixteen years later when Republican Candidate **Ronald Reagan** gave his infamous **"State's Rights"** speech in **Philadelphia, Mississippi**, which y'all can read here and listen here. Essentially, Reagan was playing on the notion that Southern states broke from the Union and created the Confederacy, which caused the **Civil War** because they didn't want the Federal government telling them that they couldn't have slaves. From this moment, the term, "state's rights," has been a symbol if not a "dog whistle" for white supremacists to assert that they should not be and would not be bound by federally mandated civil rights laws since the 1857 ***Dred Scott*** **Decision** mandated that "[African Americans] had no rights which the white man was bound to respect." With this one allegorical or symbolic speech, Reagan secured the Dixie-crat vote and the South for the Republicans. What's most evil about Reagan's speech is that it was delivered in the city where one of the most heinous hate crimes occurred—the murder of three civil rights workers: **James Chaney, Andrew Godman**, and **Michael Schwerner,** which captivated a nation and became more fuel for **Freedom Summer.** In 1980, Reagan stood on the ground where this murder occurred and invited the murderers and those who sanctioned and supported that murder into the Republican Party, which gave the Republican Party a major increase in political power. Because of this, whites who remained Democrats, for a myriad of reasons, have been running scared ever since, always trying to balance themselves between a solid black base and luring as many kinda or not-so-racist whites to the party. This type of agenda gets you a

President Bill Clinton victory only because he's willing to propose an asinine and racist crime bill to convince enough white voters, especially Southern white voters from six states, that he's not a threat to provide full citizenship to black people. Yet, it must be said that there were more than enough local and national black folks who were demanding that something be done about the crack epidemic, which was spurring crime to an all-time high. A good number of black folks supported that crime bill because a drowning man will reach for anything, even a sword. But, my pops—a certified youth court counselor who cut the recidivism rate of his cases in half by creating parenting classes rather than working to put young people in jail—was one of the very few folks, black or white, who was saying publically, even then, that incarceration is not the proper solution to the crack epidemic. However, once again, black folks chose the lesser of two evils simply because Clinton was a better choice than incumbent **President George H. W. Bush.** During the 1992 Democratic Primary, I loudly supported and voted for California **Governor Jerry Brown** because of his education plan, his support of labor unions, his creation of a surplus in the California budget, and his considering **Jesse Jackson** as his VP. But, despite these accomplishments, Brown was deemed too liberal, which is odd since *The American Conservative* stated that he was "much more of a fiscal conservative than Governor Reagan." Unfortunately, Brown's willingness to consider Jackson as a running mate and being perceived as soft on crime, which means that he was not willing to use the prison industrial complex to create and maintain the new Jim Crow, meant that he couldn't secure enough swing, Southern, or conservative white votes to win a national election.

Folks must understand this history and the fragile mentality of many white democrats to understand why so many of them went running scared after **President Joe Biden**'s poor debate with former **President Agent Orange**. Let me be clear. The Democrats got punked into making **Vice President Kamala Harris** their nominee for President in the same way that **President Barack Obama** was only handed the keys to the ship after **President George W. Bush** had crashed the U.S. Titanic into the housing-bubble iceberg. Y'all don't have to take my word for it. Take the word of Texas Representative **Jasmine Crockett** who wrote, "Well I hope the geniuses that pushed the most consequential President of our lifetime out, have a plan. WHO in the hell couldn't sell the MF Accomplishments & win over a 34 time convicted Felon who isn't even allowed to operate businesses in the state of NY (and therefore should automatically be disallowed from say running the country) & his ENTIRE team IS project 2025?! Joe wasn't the problem... dems were" (here). Or, take the word of sports journalist and cultural critic **Jemele Hill** who was one of the first public persons to challenge President Agent Orange on his racism as she stated that the overly anxious if not cowardly Democrats "turned on Biden" because the Republicans continually have them running scared (here). And, as Hill rightly states, many of the major Democrat donors didn't support Harris' presidential campaign and made it public that they wouldn't support her as the replacement for Biden. Even longtime activist and former Dean of the **Jackson State University College of Education Dr. Ivory Phillips** published the insightful article, **"It's not so much about Joe Biden; It's about Democracy,"** which can be found here. Now, most dumbasses will read all of this and say, "Oh, you ain't supporting Harris, and you didn't support Obama?" But, as I indicate, only a dumbass will ask me that. So, rather than respond to those dumbasses, I'll just have y'all read my record here or watch it here. My point is, to quote JSU athletic historian **Zo Phillips**, two things can be true. Once again, the Democratic Party is in disarray, and, once again, a black person is being asked to clean the mess. And, I'm not opposed to us doing this because, regardless of what I think of America, I still live here. While my **DD214** with **"Honorable Discharge"** on it is meaningless, I still must work to repair this raggedy-ass American house because no one else will repair it for me. As novelist and poet **Alice Walker** stated, "We are the ones for whom we are waiting." Let me be even clearer. To paraphrase poet, playwright, novelist, and activist **Kalamu ya Salaam**, there has never been any real decency, democracy, or Christianity in America until black folks worked collectively to force white folks to fulfill their empty rhetoric. That's the real legacy of black folks in America, which was evidenced when Mississippi native **Stacey Abrams** delivered Georgia by delivering Atlanta to the Democrats. Yet, this was also just seen this week when black folks galvanized the Democratic

Party by raising millions of dollars for Harris' campaign, such as **Win with Black Women** raising 1.5 million dollars in three hours (here) and **Roland Martin** and the **Star Network** hosting a call that raised 1.2 million donated mostly by black men (here). Despite all the hell that has and continues to happen to us, most black folks remain committed to working to help America fulfill its utopian creed about democracy because most of what's great about America has been built on the backs and creativity of black folks. Furthermore, we've often helped lift America from its mess with one hand tied behind our backs even when it was America who bound us.

By the time the 2020 Democratic Primary rolled into Mississippi, Harris, then in South Bend, IN, **Mayor Pete Buttigieg**, and businessman **Andrew Yang** had withdrawn from the race, leaving me with the slim pickings of Biden, **Bernie Sanders**, and **Tulsi Gabbard**. I closed my eyes, pointed my pencil, and it found Sanders' bubble. I didn't think that Sanders had a snowball's chance in hell to win the presidency, but his agenda most aligned with mine. I also hoped that a strong showing by Sanders would influence the policies of Biden's presidency. Thus, after Biden won the primary, I voted for him in the general election—not because he was the best choice for me or my community but because he wasn't the worst. Now, we stand at another fork in the constantly winding and crooked road of American poli-tricks. And, once again, black people are being asked to save the Democratic Party. Moreover, we're being asked to save the soul of America. The racist and greedy white folks keep driving the damn U.S. Titanic into icebergs created by themselves, and black folks are always there to salvage the wreckage. That statement is not to discount millions of white liberals, which includes union supporters, fully funding education supporters, DEI supporters, pro-choice supporters, healthcare reform supporters, police reform supports, judicial reform supporters, immigration reform supporters, gun reform supporters, the LGBTQ+ community, and more. It just seems that, once again, white America is forced to play the second-string quarterback who probably should have been the starting quarterback all along. In the words of *SNL* legend **Maya Rudolph** comically portraying Harris withdrawing from the 2020 Democratic Primary, "...America...You withheld your donations, and I got tired of waiting. So, I walked my fine ass out the door. You could have had a bad bitch" (here). Well, now, America has a second chance to support a good woman, and we better make the most of it because good women usually don't wait for trifling dudes to get their ish together.

I won't act like I agree with every decision or move that Attorney General or VP Harris has made. (I was critical of President Obama sanctioning the murder of **Muammar al-Gaddafi** and his initial defunding of HBCUs [here], but I never stopped supporting his efforts to make democracy a real thing in America.) Thus, voting for VP Harris will be one of the few times that, when I'm casting my ballot, I know that this candidate has no intent to harm the black community. And, that's not because she's a black woman or an **HBCU** graduate. While I was too young to vote at the time, **President Jimmy Carter** remains my favorite U.S. President because there was nothing in his policies that was designed to limit or harm black people. I just hate that his religious beliefs wouldn't allow him to kill people who took American hostages, which opened the door to Reagan becoming President. However, based on what we know, VP Harris won't have that same conflict of faith as she seems more than capable of dealing with foreign nations who desire to play hardball with the U.S. Besides, history has shown us—whether it's **Ella Baker**, Hamer, Abrams, **Sojourner Truth, Ida B. Wells-Barnett, Dorie Ladner, Mary McLeod Bethune, Shirley Chisholm, Harriet Tubman, Constance Slaughter-Harvey, Michelle Obama, Angela Davis, Ketanji Brown-Jackson, Monica McInnis, Assata Shakur, Mae Jemison, Barbara Jordan,** or many more—black women don't crumble or run and hide from adversity. (For more on this, read the poem, **"For Our Women,"** here.)

We all know that America is facing a fight for its life. Although I disagree with how the Democrats went about preparing for this fight, I agree that they have chosen the right fighter. As President Biden stated, "...nothing, nothing can come in the way of saving our democracy. That includes personal ambition" (here). If he can put aside his ego and ambition for the sake of democracy, I can continue to work around the flaws and failings of political parties for the greater good. VP Harris is clearly the more intelligent and the more humane of the two candidates. Most importantly, she's the sanest. So, I'mma do what millions of black folks have done before me—vote for the best alternative to keep the Confederates at bay while continuing to work to create a more sovereign way of life for black peoples. We might be living in **Prince**'s dystopian **"Future,"** surrounded by several **"Sign 'O' the Times,"** but **"We March"** with our **"Black Muse"** so that **"America** [will] keep the children free..." under the mantle of "Freedom...Love...Joy...Peace!"

Grass
Cheryl Caesar

"'I don't know -- I don't care. Somehow you will fail.
Something will defeat you.
 Life will defeat you." - Winston Smith in George Orwell's
1984

"I am the grass.
 Let me work." - Carl Sandburg

And there he sits,
or tilts like an officious grasshopper
over the wooden podium.

Face sprayed to fake the sun,
hair shellacked to cheat the wind,
he rails against Marxists and the Green New Deal.

And all the while his mutinous lungs,
refusing to hoard their molecular billions,

are taking in oxygen according to their needs,
and returning carbon dioxide to the best
of their ability, to every blade of grass:
golf course and garbage heap, indifferently.

(Previously published in *Writers Resist,* August 2024.)

The occupied
Cheryl Caesar

It's no longer the fear
of being cornered,
blinded with bear spray
and beaten with the poles of their strange flags;

no longer, or not only, the terror
of being gunned down
or circled with torches like a witch
or a dangerous book;

it's the accumulating dread
of invasion, penetration, contamination,
like the hundred thousand particles of microplastic
said to colonize every human body,

by the toxins we absorb each day,
washed down with phrases like *the new normal*
and *shocked but not surprised*;
infection by a noxious ideology. By now

I can see them, a dirty cloud
each time I exhale. Seeping yellow
and stinking from my pores. Polluting
even my tears, the ones that still can flow.

Aftermath
Cheryl Caesar

On the first day our Facebook pages went black.
We drove to work through a film of tears
and hugged each other in the hallways, unashamed,
and in the women's room. We talked about renewing passports,
and families in Canada. We avoided referring
to the beginning of *The Handmaid's Tale*. We went
on to meet our classes, or conference with students
who complained, "I didn't know
this assignment would be so evidence-based."
We kept our blurry eyes front, and flowed
through the day on a current of work and love.

On the second day, we posted galaxies and poems
of resistance on Facebook, and the numbers
of suicide hotlines. And Joplin's "Solace" was playing
on WKAR on the way in, and the sun
reached a few gentle fingers through the clouds.
So at work we taped the resistance poems
to the inside stall doors in the women's room.
In the halls we wondered how the Refugee
Development Center was doing, how we could help.
We went on to conference with students who said,
"I just kinda smushed two facts and two sources
together," for the sake of convenience.

And we slept several hours each night, albeit
with Ambien, which we had been off for three months.
And now I have to admit that I have no idea
whether anyone has gone back on Ambien but me.
But it feels so much better, stronger, safer, to say "we,"
like Offred in *The Handmaid's Tale*, explaining,
"We put the butter on our skin." She had no idea either.
But a friend had posted on Facebook, "This is no reason
to break your sobriety," so I know others are tempted
to temporary oblivion, and I kind of smush
the facts together. Which is I guess
a definition of fiction. On Monday I will see

the fact-smushing student, and tell him, "So maybe research
is not your jam. Maybe you prefer
fiction. But in these times, submerged in a flood
of information, wouldn't it be good to have a few tools
to tell the difference?" I hope it will work. I hope
he still believes in some kind of truth. Yesterday he wrote,
"I used a reliable source but the facts were wrong. I learned
not to trust the internet."
(Previously published in *Across the Margin*, 11 November 2024.)

Portrait of Frances Perkins
Cheryl Ceaser

The charcoal drawing represents Frances Perkins, the first woman ever to serve in the cabinet of an American president (Roosevelt). She was Labor Secretary and one of the creators of the Social Security program, now under threat by Trump and Musk.

It must be...
William Khalipwina Mpina

It must be an idea, coming not from man,
It must be the gods smiling upon Mother Earth.
It must be the tides rising, pulled by forces undetected.
It must be a shadow moving, shifting across the skies.
It must be the chains, breaking under their own weight.
It must be a new order, spoken not in words but in motion.
It must be the whispered echoes of democracy, collapsing into silence or rising anew.
It must be the falling walls of division, fading into dust.
It must be the tariffs unbreaking, their grip tightening, or loosening with time.
It must be the borders closing, forever rigid, or bending to the will of the people.
It must be a global wave, rising to erase the established policies, or to redefine them.
It must be the vows collapsing, east and west, north and

south, or reforged in unity.
It must be an eagle flying, its wings strengthened by political muscles, yet questioning its course.
It must be the voice of Donald Trump, against everything EAST, or the chorus of many voices seeking balance.
It must be a force not born of war, nor built on fear, but of collective will.
It must be artificial intelligence, weaving a new fabric, challenging the old threads of power.
It must be ancient dreams of equality, reshaped by hands unseen.
It must be the local markets bowing, their ledgers turned to ash, or rising from it.
It must be a revolution, returning with a quiet fury, demanding answers: is democracy dead, dying, or alive?
It must be the firm now bankrupt, swaying with the wind, or rebuilding from its foundations.
It must be new trade beginning, endless and unbroken, or fractured by the weight of greed.
It must be the new idea, coming not from man, but from the collective breath of humanity.
It must be growth, it must be change, for US all— questioning, evolving, enduring.

And gods have never slept
William Khalipwina Mpina

And gods have never slept, their breath the air humanity inhales.
And gods have never slept, their hands guiding minds to unlearn and unmind.
And gods have never slept, their vision shaping roots of hatred or healing.
And gods have never slept, their will replacing weeds with seeds of renewal.
And gods have never slept, their touch turning water into wine, scarcity into abundance.
And gods have never slept, their whispers turning buds into signs of hope.
And gods have never slept, their hum filling streets like the buzz of restless bees.
And gods have never slept, their nectar flowing freely, unbound by borders or nations.
And gods have never slept, their voices rustling through trees and streams, ancient yet eternal.
And gods have never slept, their dreams weaving trade through the land, connecting all.
And gods have never slept, their strength breaking iron chains of merchants and tyrants alike.
And gods have never slept, their light spreading like stars in a cosmic dance of creation.
And gods have never slept, their breath giving life to forests, to trees that stand tall.

And gods have never slept, their branches wide, sheltering all who seek refuge beneath.

And gods have never slept, their hands planting millions of seeds, millions of possibilities.

And gods have never slept, their care tending to the world's ever-shifting needs.

And gods have never slept, their gaze banishing blight and decay, restoring balance.

And gods have never slept, their dawn blooming the future in soft, golden light.

And gods have never slept, their rivers running where trade was once caged, now free.

And gods have never slept, their choices mysterious, giving us Donald Trump again—a test, a trial, a mirror.

And gods have never slept, their presence eternal, their purpose unfolding in ways we may never fully understand.

Show me, don't tell me...
William Khalipwina Mpina

Show me, don't tell me—
a river cuts through silence,
its currents bound by hidden hands.
It gives, it takes, it disappears,
like democracy's pulse—faint, yet persistent.
Gates open wide, cups rise,
beneath the eye that sees but does not blink.
Is it alive, or is it a mirage?
Dams rise on distant shores,
their floodgates turned by strangers,
while voices rise and banners fall.
The river bends, the village waits.
Some drink deeply, some scrape the bottom,
some build walls to claim its flow.
Chains hide in the gift,
their weight disguised as freedom.
Rivers break, power shifts,
but the land remains—
a witness to the ebb and flow of promises.
Those who dig their own wells
never thirst, they say,
but what of those without the tools?
Show me, don't tell me—
is democracy the river,
or the hands that divert its course?

Is it the flood that nourishes,
or the drought that starves?
Dig yours, leave mine,
says the voice of division.
That's Donald Trump,
on his second coming—
a storm cloud over the river,
claiming to protect its flow
while damming it for a chosen few.
Show me, don't tell me—
is democracy dead,
its body carried by the current?
Is it dying, gasping for air
beneath the weight of greed?
Or is it alive,
its roots stubbornly clinging
to the riverbed,
waiting for the next tide to rise?

How Trump Tried To Bully African Countries With Used Clothes
Charlie R. Braxton

Now that America's 2024 presidential election is over, and Donald Trump has emerged victorious, many foreign pundits are pontificating on what this means to the international community. Each nation is concerned about what Trump's policies will do for their particular country. Will he harm or help them?

As an African-American Pan-Africanist, my concern is what Trump's aggressive tariffs will mean for countries on the African continent. Will it be good or bad for them? As of now, no one knows the exact answer. However, if history is the best barometer for predicting the future, then I believe he will use tariffs to bully African countries into doing what's best for American business interests. Using the US's economic leverage to bully a smaller country is exactly how the Trump administration dealt with Africa during his first term in office when there was a dispute over used clothes with African countries like Ghana and Rwanda.

This incident started with Trump's Prosper Africa initiative. According to the Congressional Research Service, Trump's program called Prosper Africa "aims to unleash the U.S. unmatched competitive advantages to vastly accelerate" U.S.-Africa trade and investment, including by creating "a pipeline of U.S.-Africa trade and investment opportunities" for U.S. firms active in the region. It seeks to do so, in part, by helping to facilitate business transactions and "blended finance solutions to de-risk investment opportunities" and by supporting business-facilitating regulatory and policy reforms and environments in Africa..."

While Trump's Prosper Africa initiative was big on fostering business opportunities for American companies seeking business opportunities in Africa, it fell short of offering Africa the kind of substantial aid it needed to develop properly. Trump's bilateral push to open up markets and services could potentially hurt smaller African countries like Benin and Lesotho's economic growth because their markets weren't big enough to merit separate trade deals with the US. To make matters worse, the Trump Administration added punitive measures against countries that refused to adhere to the Administration's narrow reciprocal idea of "free trade." Such punitive measures were placed on Rwanda for placing a hefty tax on, of all things, used clothes imported from the U.S. Rwanda did this to protect its textile industry, which was being devastated by the importation of second-hand clothes. Many African countries, like Ghana, Kenya, Uganda, and Tanzania, have also seen a sharp decline in their domestic textile industries since market liberalization, which led to a drastic decrease in textile jobs.

According to the BBC's Tara John, many African nations were once the home of a thriving textile industry that is dwindling in part due to the import of foreign garments. "Second-hand clothing is one factor in the near-collapse of the garment industry in sub-Saharan Africa," writes John. "The West's cast-offs were so cheap that local textile factories and self-employed tailors could not compete." So by imposing tariffs on used garments, they would cost more than locally made clothes, thus enticing Rwandans to buy more locally made clothes. In turn, this would've boosted their textile market, bringing much-needed textile jobs to Rwandans. Essentially, Rwanda was trying to gradually phase second-hand US clothes out of their market.

This move infuriated the US-based organization called the Secondary Materials and Recycled Textiles Association (SMRTA), which relied on the African market for 13% of its overall revenue. The East African Community (EAC), which includes Rwanda, comprised a significant portion of SMRTA's African profits. SMRTA lobbied the Trump Administration for help resolving the matter, and, he retaliated by lifting the tax-free status of Rwandan textiles imported to the U.S. Rwanda enjoyed this tax-free status under the African Growth and Opportunity Act (AGOA).

It is important to note that Rwanda isn't the only country in the EAC to impose textile tariffs on US garments. Other East African countries, like Kenya, Uganda, and Tanzania, all made efforts to ban U.S. secondhand clothes from their countries. However, the threat of being removed from AGOA's tax-free status was enough to make Kenya, Uganda, and Tanzania back down. This left Rwanda the proverbial last man standing in a trade war with the U.S., and Rwanda's President, Paul Kagame stood firm in his conviction. While Trump's tariffs hurt Rwanda's wounded textile industry even more, costing the country's garment workers even more jobs it strengthened the country's resolve to expand their textile industry, as well as increase the desirability of Chinese textile goods, which are cheaper than American used clothes. In the long run, Rwanda can reestablish its textile industry and expand the international market for their textile goods. In that case, Rwanda may become economically stronger on the other side of this trade war. Either way, Kagame's move on this matter is pragmatic and his resolve admirable.

On the other hand, Trump's reaction toward Rwanda's textile industry certainly didn't win him any friends in Rwanda or the rest of Sub-Saharan Africa. Not only did Trump use his economic power to browbeat a country that's smaller and poorer than the U.S. into adopting a policy that was killing their textile industry, he did so arbitrarily. For example, Brazil has some of the most restrictive trade measures, according to a 2018 report by the European Commission (EC). US businesses have faced heavy restrictions and tariffs when trying to trade with Brazil, but the Trump Administration did not engage in a trade war with Brazil. Nor did he engage in one with India, whose tariff rate was among the highest of any major economy. He did, however, engage in a heated trade war with China, which ended in a stalemate with the U.S. economy taking heavy losses. According to a report published by the Brookings Institute, the US/China trade war "significantly hurt the American economy without solving the underlying economic concerns that the trade war was meant to resolve." It is an open secret that Donald Trump has disdain for Africa and the Caribbean. The American media reported that Trump once referred to Haiti and other African nations as "shithole countries." These crude, racist remarks drew condemnation from leaders around the world, including leaders from many African and Caribbean nations, and placed further strain on the US's tenuous relationship with Africa and the rest of the Global South. This tension carried over to the Joe Biden Administration, which was saddled with the task of repairing relations with Africa. This was critical considering China is making significant strides in establishing economic ties in Africa. The reason why China's presence in Africa made the U.S. uneasy was because they knew China's economic investments afforded them political influence in Africa. The same is true for Russia, which is also making strategic inroads in Africa.

Biden's administration understood the strategic importance of shoring up the US relationship with Africa, although he wasn't above using America's economic might as leverage against African countries as well. Africa is the richest continent on the face of the Earth. It has a bountiful amount of oil, lithium, cobalt, gold, and a plethora of other metals and minerals that are vital to the US economy. These raw materials make Africa an important player in the U.S.'s game of global dominance. If the U.S. is to retain its strategic relationship with Africa, it needs a President who fully comprehends Africa's vital role in America's economy. The president must be willing to treat Africa with the same deference it treats any of its Western European allies: with mutual respect. What is definitely not needed is a President who sees African countries as nothing more than "shitholes" to be bullied and, exploited, this would be unacceptable. Africa has been the victim of this kind of international coercion by the U.S. and other Western power for decade. It's time for the continent to stand up and put a stop to it. I believe that a truly united Africa would put a halt to this kind of international bullying.

LIBERTY'S LAMENT TO THE GILDED TYRANT
Emman Usman Shehu

I am she who stands on the rock of ages
torch ablaze   my copper heart unyielding

I   Libertas   mother of exiles   whose tablet bears
the birth-cry of a nation   You   orange-crowned

narcissist   squatting in the house of the people
What have you done to my name?   What have you
made of my flame?   Your tongue   a serpent's coil

spits venom on the tired   the poor   cages children
at borders   builds walls where bridges should rise

You call my huddled masses VERMIN   Yet I welcomed
your own kin   from distant shores to this harbor's

embrace   Have you forgotten   man of gold-plated lies?
Your chaos is a storm that shakes my robe   your dictates
chains forged anew   your dishonesty   a fog that dims

my torch   Felon   you parade as king   your scepter
a tweet   your crown a cap   Yet I   Liberty   have seen

empires fall   Pharaohs   Caesars   and tin gods like you
In the shadow of my gaze   I watched slaves break iron

bonds   suffragists claim their vote   Marchers cross
bridges stained with blood   You   who mocks justice
with pardons for cronies   who wields power

like a butcher's blade   Know this   my light outlasts
your reign   From Lagos to Harlem   my sisters sing

Their voices weave a chain you cannot break   We
the wretched   the dreamers   the free   will rise

where your towers crumble   Step down   false prophet
of liberty's name   For I am the mother who endures
My torch   a fire no tyrant   can quench

My truth   a tide no lie   can drown

THE NEW AGENT ORANGE
Emman Usman Shehu

In the land of the eagle   where dreams
once took wing   a shadow creeps low

with a venomous sting   He is Agent Orange
not of barrels but breath   sowing seeds

of discord   harvesting death   His tongue
a sprayer   dioxin of lies   each word a blight
burning truth where it flies   Fields of reason

wither, trust curls to ash   unity's roots choke
in his poisonous splash   With a crown of gold

hair   he strides through the fray   instilling
fear's fog   turning night into day

"Believe only me!" cries his carnival roar
while facts rot   like crops on a war-torn shore
Disorder's his dance   chaos his art   he splinters

the soul of a nation's heart   Brother turns
on brother   neighbor on kin   His laughter

the cackle of a Kremlin-born sin   Is he pawn
or puppeteer   this man of no shame?   A Russian

asset cloaked in liberty's name?   He salts the earth
of his country's creed   feeding foreign vines
with America's need   Oh   Agent Orange

your stain lingers long   a dirge for the just   a tyrant's
song   The eagle weeps   her wings heavy with grime

yet hope whispers still in the pulse of our time
We'll uproot your thorns   we'll cleanse your blight

with truth as our rain   with justice our light
For the land of the free will not bow to your reign
Agent Orange shall fall   and healing remain

She Loves You, Yeah, Yeah.....And You Know That Can't Be Bad: Al E.'s Equation Was Too Square, Hers Rocks-- 'L(ove) T(aken)=L(uv) M(ade)
Joseph B Pravda

I'm going to tell it as it was told to me; the teller of the story claimed she was finishing a well-planned stay at a kibbutz; her time was up, and she got the yen to write about her experiences living abroad, and to enlarge her worldview by winding her way through unlikely places hoping to pen a piece for 'Rolling Stone' (she's a struggling musician) or some travel zine having to do with the enduring Nature...ahem, of The Beatles.

==

She's in the African desert, Namibia--think Jack (only, Jacqueline) Nicholson in Michaelangelo Antonioni's 'The Passenger', and her Jeep's broken down. Like him, she's in the hands of a master with so high a name as to reassure her of finding the beauty buried underneath Nature's tawny rough-hewn surfaces she's about to encounter, including melanistic skin worn by humans in these parts.

She meets up with a fellow in a kind of personal oasis; it's not much, but he's got water.

"It seems trite, looking back so very far, but that Teacher in the Book was right, ain't no new trips, only trippers" the one known locally as Father McCartney muses as he addresses his trippy tribe consisting of goats, the occasionally curious--and thirsty--Muslim, and her. (I learn that a bunch of those critters is called a trip, although his innocent suggestion hinted that hers was beginning to look very much like a 'foolish trip', whereupon she proceeded to imitate a goat's bleating, revealing that she too knew the fitting name fora number of goats).

"Especially here in the desert--nothing new under   " and his bony index finger shoots a heil-like gesture of reverence to the relentless unblinking eye under whose gaze all chase either wisdom or folly, or a little of both 'chasing wind', as he chapter and verse quotes the old biblical Ecclesiast himself, said by exegetes to be Solomon himself.

A Jewess, she cynically retorts that given her secondhand knowledge of motherhood she never understood why all the fuss by those two women was necessary--or necessarily true--and/ or why either of them objected to his reported solution,

Even if kids were as valuable and useful as their sharing nicknames of goats. "Talk about bad trips..." she blurts. She's a postmodern skeptic concerning 'nothing new under the Sun'--as if they had all the modern inconveniencing industrial machines changing things for the worse back when goats occasionally farted methane gas and old Sol (the man, not that orange blob that's supposedly seen it all) had his wiser minions invent incense.

A rare sort for a missionary indeed was this African from America; he'd come to Namibia unlike another' misinformed' Richard Blaine in search of 'the waters', rather, inspired in the 60's by Dr. King's soul and The Beatles' eastward enlightenment promises.

"Out here, when I first tried to baptize folks they said they were Muslims, mainly because of Allah's natural ways." He smiled as he spoke, something she'd noticed about those who dwelt in oriental places, a kind of defensive humility or, more likely, the body's way of acknowledging the absurdity of one's immediate circumstance.

In McCartney's case at least, his reference to alleged holy ways had to do with local beetles, the kind he points to inviting her to join him nearer the parched earth on comfortable haunches sat upon by countless human generations way before Bauhaus, even chairs.

"You see..." he figuratively asks not only her eyes, but her mind, and she does; the also black creature pointed to was tuned in to the places where the rocks experience faint Atlantic-inspired pregnant clouds depositions of rolling fog's moisture, the beetles' anterior rearing skyward posed as

Nature's own dependable midwives, their architectonic backs facing a befogged makeshift operating theatre, as it were, those backs finely glistening with stud-like bas relief bumps and watertight intaglio-ed indentations as if intended to gratefully channel sweated droplets into and around their otherwise rock-filled mouths.

Herself-described Beatles air guitar pantomime is true to both THE Nature, and hers--a personal version of rock and rolling. She enters this in her official-looking Moleskin reporter's notebook--with the vertical flap, and the elastic band she displays for me as if it makes her heiress to Hemingway's way--tip of the hat to the uncertain author of the oldest bestseller.

"So, as you have seen, the Muslim-leaning would-be flock who introduced me to this...performance, as you have enacted it, they have shown me the Lord's way of finding that with which my baptistry rites require--invisible waters!"

He laughs a laugh such as might awaken the dead, of whatever faith, perhaps no longer alive for having ignored the wise beetles message. Slightly amending her skeptic's take on Solomon's 'been there, done that' epistle, she allows that mom Nature adapts, so what--She makes the wind those wise and foolish humans chase, more impressed by so-called 'dumb' animals knowing how to adapt--if that's not new it's at least flexible.

"The loving water you take is equal to the lessons of nature you make" she, now smile-laughs and he joins her, their fivefold hands fingers now folding in the cohesive way of the mighty water molecule (she digresses to some science lesson about things that stick together, like her shirt to her chest, and how everything is energy, matter, just vibrating at different frequencies, adding that I should ask Al, then, footnotes her take on general relativity: 'see, matter tells the universe to curve, the universe shoots back, telling matter to move...like we better, move on.')

He then invites this young American woman to drink of the cistern whose modern design concerns her.

"Everything old new again" he Ecclesiasts, they, now seated under the shade of a lean-to near a circle of rocks surrounding an equally thirsty singular bush. 'Copying nature', she thinks in the sing- song key of mockery.

"Have you heard of the Japanese Zen koan about the invisible hand between fingers?" he Suzukis--- "Beginners mind, many possibilities, but in the experts there are few."

She prefers to always appear the beginner, eschewing mentioning Shunryu's book in her backpack, replies that there is no spoon (she said she thanked Morpheus).

"Bingo--the kid, he got your goat, eh; our senses are poor sketchers, so the Zen is that your' seen' fingers are interlaced with those of the unseen."

She realizes what the beetles they'd watched knew, with or without Zen, or Neo.

"So, I guess your Teacher says that gizmo's old, right?" she wisecracks, risking being labeled both a spouter as well as a chaser of the wind.

Addressing her as grasshopper with none in which to hop, he just smiles, the body language of the koan, and hands her a book.

"Don't worry, not a single hymn in there."

She reads aloud, scientific gospel, via Columbia University's Earth Institute:

"Fog or dew collection is an ancient practice. Archaeologists have found evidence in Israel of low circular walls that were built around plants and vines to collect moisture from condensation. In South America's Atacama Desert and in Egypt, piles of stones were arranged so that condensation

Could trickle down the inside walls where it was collected and then stored."

She looks up, beholds McCartney's smirking face, his hand seeming to baptize his forehead from the contents of a black container logo-ed 'FogQuest.org'.

"Headline from The Daily Gleaner: Fogstand Beetles Make Comeback of Millennium" he booms, footnoting Fogstand, slang for our little water gleaner.

She decides not to blame Yoko for the very need for any comeback thanking her oriental Zen awareness. She laughs a throwaway comment about the Brit rock band Foghat on stage. "Let's just say that her invisible digits had always been bound to John's--- it was in their very   nature" he sooth-says.

She flashbacks to a film review she's reread recently, about Michaelangelo Antonioni: "...man is uneasy, something is bothering him..." From the 60's to now, his films treating of the disappearance of seemingly endless possibilities, gone in modern life. Yet, Nature, like Father McCartney's Teacher, always knew this. She digresses to Yoko, to Zen, to a college haiku: "Silent whispering, from the cocoon, butterflies, somehow, know what to do."

Reverie ends, I guess it's the heat that took her, you and me   there.

"Things, unlike us, seem to know what to do" McCartney says, passing her the jug-like receptacle. "Only, what happens to the world if the things that have always known what to do disappear, like our little friend, and no more moist low clouds?"

She gets it, he's right---that clever koan, the haiku. Waste not

Newton, 'matter's neither created nor destroyed' 17 syllables, conservative, like Nature, maybe even Yoko.

"I'm Jewish, but I feel baptized, you?" she downloads from her jangling CPU (that's what she calls her neck-top, her cabeza, the Spanish, a bow to her Sephardic heritage, throwing in 'Chris Colombo, the converso whose fam split for Genoa, man'). McCartney suggests she tell that to the thousands who annually converge on Columbus Square waving Italian flags, reading her mind, the word 'habit' underscored, then 'bad' and 'why we don't know what to do', then 'till it's too late.'

"Have a salt tablet, don't drink too much too quickly" he counsels, motioning her to his tent where they sit Arab style, sharing some sweet tea, dates.

"The tea you may thank the beetles for" as he volunteers his taken name, Michaelangelo.

"My Christian name, Pablo--my mother was Mexican--but I took the Italian's name for how it fall upon the ear."

He goes on to explain that, as by The Beatles, he was drawn by the artist's description of truest art as the shadow of divine perfection. "Since I was already the shade of shadow, I decided to take my art wherever it was truly needed--here" broadly smiling such that his mouth in this upside down world of his might itself afford ample shade to the myriad in need of it.

"The Canadians, with a third of the world's potable supply of water, came up with this, pretty cool, eh?" his last utterance clearly mock Canuck, innocently intoned.

And like a sermon surmounting a steep climb toward natural 'know-how' she, and in turn, you and I are feted to the Word, and it is good.

"Listen to the Earth speaking, through Her Institute in New York:"

'Today nearly two people in ten have no source of safe drinking water, most of them children But in some desert areas, where there is very little rain, fog and dew are abundant sources of humidity that are being harvested to produce fresh water.'

Pablo, Michael, those children's angel, along with those Canadians and lots of others like the late Matthew Power, a journalist, reveals the 'human truth' 'neath 'sorry facts'-- he tells her about how he was doing some gardening work in Los Angeles, 1967ish, up in the Hollywood Hills, place called Blue Jay Way. He hears this organ, some guy singing, just singing about the weather. Then he starts singing this Beatles tune:

'There's a fog upon L.A.,
And my friends have lost their way. "We'll be over soon," they said.
Now they've lost themselves instead...'

ASIDE TO READER: Yep, 'The Beatles Bible' verifies this, how its pedestrian roots have been supplanted by mystical overtones fogging-over George's befogged jet-lag, writing a song to kill time whilst awaiting a former band publicist's arrival (who'd called to say he was lost).

How this was his way of making some quick cash to head eastward, on his pilgrimage---that's what he called it, something about him becoming 'innocence abroad', without the sarcasm Twain gave those letters to that paper in San Francisco, with that snarky subtitle 'The New Pilgrim's Progress.' He lands in London, gets a job sweeping up a certain studio, Apple, the inspiration for Beatles-loving

Steve Jobs eponymous empire. Yes, that's where he heard what he called the second voice summoning him to go forth, and without having imbibed a fifth of any intoxicants except maybe that oriental koan's calling.

'Live a little be a gypsy, get around (get around) Get your feet up off the ground
Live a little, get around........ Heads across the sky
Hand across the water (water) Heads across the sky   '

ASIDE: He/ She, correct, 'Beatles Bible', chapter and verse, quoted:
'The final song on the 'Some Time In New York City' album, 'We're All Water' written by Yoko, a kind of meditation on the things shared among all people. He's careful to point out that he wasn't there for that one, just heard it at a friend's in London, who'd heard something similar at this art installation, from 'Water Talk', a poem which was featured in her Half-A-Wind show at the Lisson Gallery in London', the one where John first met her.
'We're all water from different rivers. That's why it's so easy to meet
We're all water in this vast, vast ocean Someday we'll evaporate together
What's the difference? There's no difference '
She believes him, and not just because he was reading them from his diary journal he keeps, "even now, especially now", he says, when and where he is learning so very much

about the why, the what, the who of 'Her', the pronoun he applies to the natural things he sees so closely.

She asks him to tell her more about these secular angels he said were rediscovering what the ancient Ecclesiast he--and the Bible--call the Teacher knew already, about the wind and those chasing it, like that butterfly in the cocoon.

He reads from an Earth Institute download on his cell phone, when he was in a monastery where they had WiFi because of their wine business:

"Fog, a cloud that touches the ground, is made of tiny droplets of water—each cubic meter of fog.

contains half the weight of a paperclip of water. Fog collectors look like tall volleyball nets slung between poles with mesh that is especially efficient at capturing water droplets. When the fog rolls in, the tiny droplets of water cling to the mesh, then drip into a gutter below that channels the water to a water tank. Fog collectors, which can also harvest rain and drizzle, are best suited to high- elevation arid and rural areas."

"There are many other great souls, nothing to do with religion, but everything to do with humility, the thing that impels them away from the old excuse that we're 'only human', and toward doing what is 'only humane'" Pablo paeans, unwitting poet who consents to her, now my, using that wonderful distinction with vast difference he claims 'just came to him'.

She tells him it reminds her of this Poe credo she'd come across at City Lights Publishing in San Francisco, in a book called 'Marginalia': "...unmasking which, also, tears away the face..."

"What else would you expect from the first detective storyteller?" I rhetoricize; Amy (otherwise still anonymous) asks me, rhetorically, "whose story" I think this is. Right.

"What about these other...souls?" she goads.

He responds by continuing to read what he seems to already have committed to memory, donning the wisdom like a fitting garment clothing his true nature.

"Scientists in Australia are developing an entirely different fog collection strategy modeled after my Stenocara beetle of this Namib Desert, one of the driest places on earth, receiving less than 2 centimeters of rain annually, so night and morning fog from the Atlantic Ocean are the lifeblood of the desert's flora and fauna..."

"Australia, using our little friends, from right here" and he begins a quiet refrain in a lovely voice she, then I've only now heard fully:

'Live a little, get around........ Heads across the sky

Hand across the water (water) Heads across the sky '

He clears his throat, unnecessarily, accentuating his rare pride. "Inspired by nature's design "

Pablo/ Michaelangelo pauses, that inverse umbrella formed by his lips shading cooling humaneness upon the facts to follow.

"...Scientists from the University of Sydney have invented a synthetic surface using a combination of chemistry and structure. The surface is composed of two layers, which makes water droplets detach as soon as they get large enough. Similar surfaces inspired by the Stenocara have collected up to 10 liters of water per square meter every hour. Prototypes have shown that this technology is several times more productive than mesh harvesting methods and could be scaled up to work in urban environments."

I blush with humility, my face of ignorance, until now, something Amy charitably agrees was her exact reaction, reminding me, again, to hit my inner mute button.

"So, Yoko was, is in good company, John & some oriental scientists..." he demonstrates his Twain- like less-than-innocent sarcasm, and continues briefly with what he calls the final part of her 'orientation', pun very much intended.

"Chinese scientists are studying the structure of spider silk to learn why it is so effective at collecting water from the air. Under an electron microscope, they've observed that spider silk fibers change structure when they come into contact with water. The scientists dipped nylon into a polymer solution; when it was stretched out, small polymer droplets formed, which became spindle knots once they dried. The scientists hope this research could potentially be used to make the Canadians' FogQuest's fog collectors even more effective."

As they looked into the other's face she, perhaps you, and certainly Michael the Angel (as I now silently regard him) a privileged sensation came over her, them, us, or so I believe; we'd had the prima facie desert's face torn away for us--perhaps by Michaelangelo's unseen feminine hand,

Hers-- Amy liked the goddess analogy, far more ancient than the Bible's Teacher--and at last beheld Her faceless countenance, a shining visage whose voiceless voice seemed to whisper in the wind chased by both the wise and the foolish: 'the love you take is equal to the love you make.'

EinstiniusGermanicusRoaminNumeralDuo
Joseph B. Pravda

Pesti/Geno-cide
Gerard Sarnat

to celebrate Gaza War day 500

This may be too much
in the weeds
say those hiding bombs and rockets
just south of Lebanon's Litani River

but in Israel —
which you may remember
at first was like on Ukraine/Russia
(trying to play both sides)

—Biden-era ago Bibi had it leaked
that they might ship captured
Hezbollah missiles to Zelenskyy...
'til Trump punctured tiny trial balloon

compared to National Holiday-level
giddiness at essentially unimaginably
humongous gift-wrapped Anything Goes
Thumbs Up US Administration support.

tanka (Trump 2.0's Riviera)
Gerard Sarnat

unilaterally –
proved to be problem -- Israel
left Gaza [I'm on
last civilian bus out] hoped
bloom oh! "Mid-East's Monaco"

BLITZKREIG 2.0
Gerard Sarnat

i. Chicken Lily-Liver [Mine White?] Liberal

Well, to start, there was a Medieval belief
that if somebody's liver is pale
he may lack real courage.

And I'll leave it to others to define Liberal.

But Gerardo has been one since six in 1951
when both my parents supported
Stevenson vs Eisenhower.

However now Sarnatzky's sorta wavering.

Not about—at times ultra—Progressivism;
yet tired of Dem leaders covering for
Biden's obvious rapid decline

no less ineffectiveness, over-regulation etc.

Oy not to point backing fascist/King Trump
though dude gets shit done: his boys
(all three) meet Putin's tomorrow.

ii.Let's Cut The Crap And Get Down To Brass Tacks

"The Moving Finger writes; and, having writ,
Moves on; nor all thy piety and wit
Shall lure it back to cancel half a line,
Nor all thy tears wash out a word of it."—*Rubaiyat,* by Omar Khayyam

Happy is the man who has broken the chains
which hurt the mind, and has given up worrying
once and for all. Be patient and tough;
one day this pain will be useful to you. –from
Metamorphoses, by Ovid

"If your intention is to care for others and to be kind,
then even when you fail, you are succeeding." —Norm
Fischer; "If you are not at the table, you're on the menu."
—what West Europe must worry about Putin/Trump 2.0.*

*https://www.nytimes.com/2025/02/16/us/politics/trump-europe-alliance-crisis.html

iii.haiku [quit politesse, begin chaos étiquette]

offered, *Join Muskrats*
-- but oy must wear hat (no tie)
in Oval Office

iv.kouta ["Double Standards," ghosted for Viktor Orbán]

Il/Liberal
"democracies"
—France, England, US
can be hypocrites—
colonize-d one
way, now preach
opposite at me.

Donald Trump au prisme de la science de Claude Bernard : entre crise démocratique et renaissance
Luc Koffi

Donald Trump through the prism of Claude Bernard's science : between democratic crisis and renaissance

Résumé : La recherche du bien-être socio-politique a amené les sociétés à adopter comme modèle universel le régime démocratique. Vue comme l'expression de la volonté du peuple et gage de la stabilité politique et économique, la démocratie connaît aujourd'hui une crise qui s'est particulièrement accentuée depuis l'accession au pouvoir de Donald Trump. Selon certains observateurs, cette ère crée un dysfonctionnement sur la scène internationale puisque le «Trumpisme» se caractérise par un nationalisme économique, une réorientation des traditionnelles relations internationales. Cependant, cette philosophie, proche de la démarche expérimentale de Claude Bernard, reste une alternative crédible pour le développement économique des États-Unis et un modèle d'émancipation pour les pays africains.
Mots-clés : Crise démocratique, émancipation, économie, science expérimentale, trumpisme
Abstract : The quest for socio-political well-being has led societies to adopt the democratic system as a universal

model, democratic system as a universal model. Seen as the expression of the will of the people and the guarantee of political and economic stability, democracy is currently experiencing a crisis that has become particularly accentuated since Donald Trump's accession to power. According to some observers, this era is creating a dysfunction on the international scene. « Trumpism" is characterized by economic nationalism, a reorientation of traditional reorientation of traditional international relations. However, this philosophy, close to Claude Bernard's experimental approach, remains a credible alternative for US economic development of the United States and a model of emancipation for African countries.

Keywords : Democratic crisis, economy, emancipation, experimental science, trumpism

Introduction

Le 20 janvier 2017 tandis que l'histoire de l'humanité semblait se tracer conformément aux aspirations des sociétés, l'investiture du 45e Président des États-Unis Donald Trump somma plus d'un. Après sa victoire à l'élection présidentielle de 2016 contre Hillary Clinton, le "milliardaire " américain alors âgé de 70 ans fit son apparition dans un univers politique hostile. Compris comme populiste et fasciste par les démocrates d'Amérique ainsi que certains États d'Europe, Donald Trump, après un mandat de gouvernement, perd les élections au profit de Joe Biden. Même s'il crie à la falsification des résultats, le natif de New-York laisse le pouvoir après quatre ans. Cependant, le 20 janvier 2025, Donald Trump est réinvesti comme 47e Président des États-Unis. Lors de l'élection présidentielle américaine de 2024, il a remporté 49, 91 % des suffrages exprimés contrairement à son la démocrate Kamala Harris qui obtient 48, 44% des voix. Cette victoire lui permet de recueillir 312 votes au collège électoral contre 226 pour son opposante.

Si la première gouvernance du Président américain est perçue par certains observateurs comme le fruit du hasard, à cause de sa politique controversée et ses relations internationales instables, cela n'est pas le cas pour son deuxième gouvernement. En effet, relativement au premier mandat de Trump, Thérèse Rebière et Isabelle Lebon pensent qu' «*au delà de son bilan, la tonalité du discours de Donald Trump a contribué à accroître les divisions existantes au sein de la société américaine* » (2020). Á en croire ces professeures de sciences économiques, le premier mandat de Donald Trump a été caractérisé par un bilan économique presqu'insignifiant. D'abord en 2016, l'économie était stable et favorable bien avant la prise du pouvoir par le parti républicain. Ensuite, face à la pandémie de la Covid 19, Trump a pris des décisions politiques qui ont effacé « *la plupart de ce qui pouvait être considéré comme ses meilleurs résultats avec une remontée spectaculaire du chômage qui atteint 14, 7% en Mai 2020* » (T. Rebière et I. Lebon, 2020).

Cependant, même si la seconde victoire à l'élection présidentielle de Donald Trump paraît surprendre de nouveau le monde politique, le peuple américain cette fois-ci semble avoir fait un choix bien réfléchi quant au gouvernement de sa destinée. Dès lors, dans quelle mesure la présidence de Donald Trump a-t-elle redéfini les dynamiques du nationalisme américain, tout en suscitant une rupture démocratique et une ère de renouveau politique ? En clair, la politique de Donald Trump vue à la lumière de la science expérimentale de Claude Bernard, propose t-elle un modèle crédible de gestion des sociétés actuelles ? Quelles sont les conséquences du nationalisme du républicain américain sur l'Europe ? Enfin, ce nouveau climat politique international offre-t-il des perspectives d'émancipation à l'Afrique ? Á partir d'une approche historique, analytique et critique, cet article se propose de s'inspirer de la rigueur scientifique de Claude Bernard pour justifier la philosophie politique de Donald Trump. Par ailleurs, il montre que la vision du Président américain, en créant un bouleversement sur la scène internationale, remet en cause les fondements de l'impérialisme et offre des perspectives de développement à l'Afrique.

I - La politique de Donald Trump et la science médicale de Claude Bernard

La philosophie politique du 45 et 47ème Président américain est résolument axée sur un nationalisme économique viril désigné par l'expression anglaise "América First " qui signifie littéralement "l'Amérique d'abord". Elle traduit la politique qui repose principiellement sur la priorité des États-Unis dans les rapports et les échanges internationaux. En plus, elle stipule que le développement des États-Unis doit s'appuyer d'abord sur la culture et les richesses économiques endogènes. Donald Trump à travers ce slogan qui situe l'absolue priorité de l'Amérique a démontré « *qu'il n'entendait aucunement respecter les engagements pris par son prédécesseur, rompant avec la règle qui prévaut de la continuité de l'État, et qu'aucune relation, fût-elle ancienne et privilégiée, ne devait échapper à un révisionnisme obsidional* » (S. Jansen, 2019). Ceci explique l'idée de la remise en cause du multilatéralisme c'est-à-dire l'organisation des relations internationales fondée sur la coopération entre les acteurs internationaux.

Cette philosophie nationaliste se rapproche des principes de la médecine expérimentale tels qu'élaborés par le physiologiste français du XIXe siècle Claude Bernard. Pour lui, la connaissance des lois de la maladie et de la santé ainsi que l'institution d'une thérapeutique crédible passent par la physiologie expérimentale. Dans ce cas, le succès de la médecine rime avec le déterminisme des propriétés endogènes. Par ce fait même il faut rappeler que l'échec de la médecine à traiter efficacement la maladie avant l'ère de Claude Bernard était dû à la méconnaissance de l'origine de la pathologie. Elle était considérée comme d'origine exogène. Pourtant, c'est bel et bien dans la physiologie que résident la pathologie et la thérapeutique. Elles « *n'avaient pas à se donner un mutuel appui dans la pratique médicale. Mais dans la conception de la médecine scientifique, il ne saurait en être ainsi ; sa base doit être la physiologie* » (C. Bernard, 1984, p. 26). En un mot, c'est d'abord dans les propriétés endogènes qu'il faut avec primauté rechercher la solution aux maux sociaux.

1 - La philosophie politique de Donald Trump

La gouvernance de Donald Trump telle que présentée par certains critiques et observateurs, apparaît comme une rupture de l'héritage politique et économique de ses prédécesseurs. En effet, George W. Bush et Barach Obama à leur arrivée au pouvoir, s'étaient inscrit dans la tradition du libre-échange entre les États-Unis et les autres pays. Mais, dès son premier mandat, Donald Trump a adopté une conception protectionniste des intérêts des États-Unis avec le slogan America first. Il a brisé l'élan du multilatéralisme en imposant des droits de douane sur certains produits tels que l'acier, l'aluminium. Il a limité l'accès de quelques entreprises chinoises au marché américain. Il s'agit entre autres de Huawai, ZTE, Tiktok etc... Si Huawei est accusé d'espionner le gouvernement américain pour le compte des chinois, la firme ZTE quant à elle, était sanctionnée d'avoir violé embargo américain contre la Corée du Nord et l'Iran. Tiktok soupçonné de collecter des données personnelles des américains afin de les transmettre au gouvernement chinois devait être vendu aux entreprises américaines. (Même si cette requête n'a pas abouti) Donald Trump « *considère que les États-Unis sont floués par leurs alliés, que l'économie mondiale joue contre les intérêts américains* » (M. Quencez, 2020).

Dès son premier mandat, le Président américain a pris la résolution de réduire la présence militaire de son pays dans le reste du monde. Depuis ce 29 mars 2025, cet engagement prend forme car il envisage un retrait partiel des formes armées américaines de l'Europe en lui laissant la responsabilité de faire face seule aux menaces militaires extérieures. Dans ce contexte,

« un document portant le nom de « Interim National Defense Strategic » (« Orientations stratégiques provisoires pour la défense nationale ») a été distribué à l'ensemble du département de la défense à la mi-mars. Signé par le nouveau secrwétaire à la défense Pete Hegseth, ce texte redéfinit les priorités de l'armée américaine en lien avec les volontés de Donald Trump. Il prévoit notamment un désengagement important de

l'armée américaine en Europe et ce même en cas d'attaque russe, rapporte The Washington Post, le 29 mars 2025.» (O. France, 2025).
Donald Trump a réduit l'implication militaire à l'étranger en retirant son pays de plusieurs accords internationaux: il a menacé l'OTAN (Organisation du Traité de l'Atlantique Nord) en demandant aux alliés de revoir à la hausse leur contribution financière. Pour contrer une éventuelle attaque russe, l'OTAN ne pourra plus désormais compter sur une quelconque aide militaire américaine. Par ailleurs, Donald Trump menace de se retirer de l'accord de Paris sur le climat. Ce traité international adopté depuis le 12 décembre 2015 durant la COP 21, répond au souci de lutter contre le réchauffement climatique. Comme objectifs, les parties lors de cette $21^{\text{ème}}$ conférence ont entendu réduire les émissions de gaz à effet de serre, atteindre un équilibre contre les émissions de carbone d'ici 2050, aider les différents états en voie de développement avec un financement minimal de cent milliards de dollars pour la transition énergétique et l'adaptation aux impacts du changements climatiques. Mais pour Donald Trump, il y a nécessité pour les états européens de payer une contribution égale à celle de son pays.

Relativement à sa politique migratoire, D. Trump a adopté une stratégie stricte visant à canaliser l'immigration légale et clandestine. « *La plus emblématique des ambitions de D. Trump demeure la construction du mur entre les États-Unis et le Mexique, qui a provoqué le plus long arrêt des activités gouvernementales (Shutdown) de l'histoire américaine.»* (M. Tardis, 5). Ce qui paraît surprenant est que l'histoire des États-Unis s'est forgée comme celle de l'immigration. C'est un continent créé à partir des migrants. Cependant, ce qui anime le Président américain, c'est sa volonté de prioriser les intérêts de ses concitoyens. Pour lui, la réduction de l'immigration permettra au gouvernement de mieux s'occuper des américains eux-mêmes. Ils pourront bénéficier de toutes les opportunités offertes par les entreprises du pays. Aussi faut-il ajouter le bien-être social des américains au cas où le phénomène migratoire venait à être jugulé.

Enfin, de formation politique conservatrice, D. Trump défend des valeurs culturelles strictement conservatrices. D'obédience chrétien protestant, il bénéficie fortement du soutien des évangéliques conservateurs. Ses prises de position sur l'avortement, les questions de genre, LGBTQ+ et de racisme démontrent que selon lui, la culture est le pilier du développement des sociétés. En effet, D. Trump est partisan de l'anti-avortement d'où sa participation à la marche pour la vie (March for life) le 24 janvier 2020) pendant son premier mandat. Relativement à la question du genre, dès son accession au pouvoir en 2025, il signe un décret reconnaissant désormais les deux (2) sexes en tant que personne: le sexe masculin et féminin. Il est également opposé aux politiques progressistes sur le racisme d'où l'interdiction des formations sur le racisme dans les agences fédérales.

Au regard de ce qui précède, la politique nationaliste de Donald Trump apparaît comme une mesure idoine pour créer les conditions d'épanouissement des américains car «*un arbre ne peut se tenir débout sans ses racines* ». (G. A. N'gbo, 2024). Et, la culture d'une nation est le fondement de son développement humain et économique. Elle doit donc s'inspirer des réalités inhérentes au peuple lui-même. Elle doit être exempte de toute influence externe. Toutefois, quel est le lien entre la philosophie politique de Donald Trump et la théorie du médecin français Claude Bernard ?

2 - La base de la médecine scientifique chez Claude Bernard

Dans les anciennes sociétés traditionnelles, la maladie et la santé avaient une origine divine car elles étaient provoquées par les entités spirituelles notamment les esprits méchants et les divinités. Cependant, si la maladie relevait de la colère des forces surnaturelles, la santé quant à elle s'obtenait par le pardon de ces mêmes forces ou esprits. C'est pourquoi, la médecine dans ses premiers pas, était l'affaire des sorciers, des chamans et des prêtres. Ainsi, *Dans les anciennes cultures tribales, la maladie était souvent considérée comme causée par des forces surnaturelles. Depuis les temps anciens, des « hommes médecine » (qualifiés de docteur, chamans ou sangomas, suivant les ethnies) ont en charge la santé de leurs populations, leurs pratiques incluent des cérémonies, de la petite chirurgie, l'utilisation de sorts et celles des plantes médicinales.* (Clifford A. Pickover, 16).

Autrement dit, vus comme des docteurs, ceux-ci prescrivaient aux malades des remèdes basés sur les incantations magiques, des cérémonies d'exorcisme ainsi que des prières. Par ce fait même, ils avaient la charge de soigner leurs populations, de veiller à leur sécurité et à leur santé. Ces docteurs étaient les premiers responsables des membres de leurs sociétés. Celles-ci tiraient donc tout leur espoir de l'autorité des médecins puisqu'ils utilisaient toutes les méthodes possibles pour maintenir leur santé. La thérapeutique des docteurs traditionnels prenait en compte les cérémonies rituelles, quelques petites pratiques relatives à la chirurgie ainsi que les plantes et des rites incantatoires. Par conséquent, le caractère exogène de la maladie et de la santé a empêché l'évolution de la thérapeutique.

Au Ve siècle avant Jésus-Christ, l'avènement du médecin grec Hippocrate de Cos permit à la médecine de se débarrasser de son caractère transcendant pour prendre un statut immanent. Ainsi, la médecine rationnelle instituée par Hippocrate était synonyme de médecine scientifique mais elle ne pouvait pas expérimenter. De ce fait, Claude Bernard reconnu la valeur du procédé d'observation dans la médecine élaborée par Hippocrate. Cependant, la science hippocratique était insuffisante pour car elle manquait de rigueur expérimentale; ensuite, elle était dépourvue de déterminisme dans l'approche du pathologique. Enfin, les principes de la thérapeutique hippocratique étaient axés sur des caractéristiques exogènes. La médecine hippocratique ne visait pas à arrêter la maladie mais à la suivre dans son développement jusqu'à son achèvement. Elle était par ailleurs contemplative car elle agissait sur les entités morbides selon l'ordre de la nature mais ne pouvait les arrêter ou les modifier. En clair, « les anciens ne connaissaient que les sciences d'observation, les sciences passives, qui permettent de prévoir les phénomènes de la nature pour les éviter ou les rechercher, mais ne donnent pas la puissance de les maîtriser » (C. Bernard, 1947, p. 87). En d'autres termes, à partir de Claude Bernard, la médecine est devenue expérimentale. Désormais, elle analyse expérimentalement les mécanismes de la maladie et de la santé. Elle n'est plus une science passive qui se contente d'observer le rôle de la nature dans le processus de guérison. La médecine expérimentale cherche à connaître tous les phénomènes physiologiques.

En outre, en nous rapportant à la biographie de Claude Bernard, nous nous rendons compte qu'il travailla

auprès d'un pharmacien appelé Louis-Joseph-Marie Millet du 1er Janvier 1832 au 30 juillet 1833 à Lyon. Durant ces dix-neuf mois, il fut très déçu des pratiques de charlatanisme et d'empirisme dont usait le pharmacien pour soigner les malades. C'est donc cette insuffisance que présentait la thérapeutique de son époque qui le poussa à envisager les fondements d'une médecine active. En instituant ainsi la médecine expérimentale, Claude Bernard visait donc l'intérêt suprême de l'homme qui est la santé. c'est pourquoi, « la médecine expérimentale est une médecine scientifique, qui est fondée sur la physiologie et qui a pour but de trouver les lois des fonctions du corps vivant afin de pouvoir les régler et les modifier dans l'intérêt de la santé de l'homme » (C. Bernard, 1984, p. 7).
La physiologie est l'étude des phénomènes vivants dans le souci de mieux cerner leur fonctionnement. En règle générale, le vivant est un être complexe constitué de cellules; il possède un métabolisme particulier qui lui permet d'effectuer des échanges d'énergie avec l'environnement extérieur. Il est également caractérisé par des phénomènes auto-regénérescence , de reproduction, de respiration etc... Il possède une organisation influençable par des facteurs tels que le climat, l'âge, le sexe et l'alimentation. Ce qui lui confère une idiosyncrasie singulière et qui semble rendre inaccessible le décryptage du vivant. Cependant, Claude Bernard pense que la

connaissance du vivant est bel et bien simple. Elle s'appuie sur le milieu intérieur caractérisé par un fluide dans lequel baignent les cellules vivantes des animaux supérieurs. Il se rapporte le plus souvent aux différents liquides internes à la vie des animaux les plus élevés en organisation. En tant qu'intermédiaire entre les échanges cellulaires organiques et le milieu extérieur, il est constitué des éléments physico-chimiques et des mécanismes anatomiques dont l'équilibre constitue l'homéostasie. Et pour Claude Bernard,

La médecine antique considéra l'influence du milieu cosmique, des eaux, des airs et des lieux ; on peut, en effet, tirer de là d'utiles indications pour l'hygiène et pour les modifications morbides. Mais ce qui distinguera la médecine expérimentale moderne, ce sera d'être fondée surtout sur la connaissance du milieu intérieur dans lequel viennent agir les influences normales et morbides ainsi que les influences médicamenteuses. (C. Bernard, 1984, pp. 149-149).

En clair, la médecine rationnelle initiée par Hippocrate de Cos voyait dans le milieu extérieur les facteurs de la maladie et de la santé. Ce qui pouvait aider à éviter certaines maladies à partir de l'hygiène. C'est ce que vient révolutionner Claude Bernard par l'institution du milieu intérieur comme principe fondamental de la médecine. Le milieu intérieur est caractérisé par différents éléments composites que sont le sang, l'eau, l'oxygène, la chaleur, les substances chimiques ou réserves. Ceux-ci entretiennent la vie en lui maintenant une constance indépendamment des influences du monde extérieur.

Par conséquent, contre les grandes théories médicales qui se sont succédé de l'Antiquité jusqu'au XIXe siècle et qui reposaient en majorité sur des principes exogènes, Claude Bernard a institué une médecine essentiellement fondée sur des bases endogènes. Cette démarche a permis à l'humanité de faire un bond dans la thérapeutique. Ce modèle scientifique est repris par Donald Trump trois siècles après. Mais, la crise de la démocratie actuelle et le balbutiement de l'Europe se justifient-ils du fait de la politique endogène du 47e Président américain ?

II - L'Europe en crise : la rupture démocratique en Europe

Un constat est évident, il s'agit de l'état actuel de la démocratie en Europe, secouée par une crise sans précédent. Cette thèse est amplement développée par le 25e Président de la république française Emmanuel Macron lors de la conférence des ambassadrices et des ambassadeurs. L'Europe tâtonne pour reconstituer une identité économique et militaire et technologique, ce qui traduit son impuissance dans le règlement du conflit entre l'Ukraine t la Russie. Enfin la montée fulgurante du populisme fait basculer les règles anciennement établies faisant de la démocratie, le régime idéal pour la liberté et l'épanouissement des populations.

1 - Le statut de la démocratie actuelle vu "le discours du Président français Emmanuel Macron lors de la 30ème conférence des ambassadrices et des ambassadeurs du lundi 06 janvier 2025"

La 30e édition de la conférence des chefs de missions diplomatiques français pour définir les grandes orientations de la politique étrangère de la France, présidée par le Président Emmanuel Macron, est marquée par une teinte particulière : la rupture démocratique en Europe. Dans un discours sous fond de crise d'un monde en désordre, le Président a dressé un tableau du mal démocratique en trois registres. D'abord, le volet stratégique prend en compte le regain des conflits armés, l'affaiblissement des normes internationales ainsi que la montée en puissance des États révisionnistes; au niveau technologique, la révolution numérique avec l'intelligence artificielle et son corollaire de désinformation. Et, sur le plan politique et philosophique, il y a le refoulement des valeurs morales et humanistes engendré par l'accroissement des régimes autoritaires et dictatoriaux.

À l'aube du XXIe siècle, après de grands espoirs entretenus sur l'évolution du monde, l'humanité se réveille brutalement avec un « *désordre né de l'affaiblissement des règles internationales, contestées par d'autres puissances qui ne jouent plus le jeu, se déploient sans complexe dans de nouveaux espaces de confrontation internationale et tentent de fragmenter le monde à leur avantage* » (E. Macron, 2025, p. 2). En effet, certaines puissances révisionnistes ne se contentent plus de gérer leurs frontières, elles veulent désormais s'étendre vers d'autres États en les annexant ou en s'ingérant dans les politiques étrangères. C'est le cas de la Roumanie, l'Allemagne et de l'Arménie respectivement victimes de l'ingérence de la Russie, les États-Unis et l'Azerbaïdjan.

Dans ce climat, la France doit donc faire face aux défis internationaux. Cela passe par le renforcement de la diplomatie française avec l'augmentation du budget du ministère en Europe et des affaires étrangères, l'adaptation aux défis nouveaux à l'exemple de l'intelligence artificielle et la multiplication de ses diplomates à l'international. Au niveau de ses relations transatlantiques, elle exprime sa volonté de continuer sa coopération avec les États-Unis et de maintenir les échanges constructifs malgré le changement de régime politique avec Donald Trump et son administration. Par ailleurs, la France traduit la nécessité pour l'Europe de maintenir sa souveraineté en matière de défense, d'économie et d'industrie. Relativement à ses priorités géopolitiques, la France envisage continuer son soutien à l'Ukraine face à la Russie. Pour le Proche-Orient, le Président Emmanuel Macron propose une solution à

deux États dans le conflit israélo-palestinien. Aussi ajoute-t-il la coopération entre la France et les pays arabes dans le but de stabiliser la région. Quant à l'Afrique, la France voudrait procéder à une réorganisation de l'armée française pour l'adaptation aux nouvelles politiques africaines dans les régions sahéliennes et subsahariennes. De ce fait,
le deuxième élément, s'appelle le Marché unique. On doit aller au bout du Marché unique pour avoir un vrai marché domestique pour nos entreprises. On a un levier de croissance formidable qui ne coûte pas un euro d'argent public, c'est de lever les barrières entre les 27 pays membres. Dans tous les domaines où ça existe déjà, on doit l'accélérer. Si on veut que nos startups, nos géants, nos champions de l'intelligence artificielle soient dans la compétition internationale, il faut juste que leur marché domestique ne soit pas le marché français, mais le marché de l'Union européenne. Approfondissement du marché européen, c'est exactement la clé aussi en matière de numérique, en matière d'énergie, de télécommunication. (E. Macron, p.11).
Autrement dit, pour que l'Europe soit un continent plus performant dans tous les secteurs, il fat un marché commun. Cette fédération rendrait tous les États plus puissants et plus autonomes que la volonté d'évoluer seul sur le marché international.

Enfin, évoquant la question des enjeux globaux, le Président Emmanuel Macron s'est prononcé sur la thématique du climat et de la démocratie. Pour lui, il convient de faire une promotion des valeurs liées au respect de l'environnement sans imposer un modèle unique. La démocratie doit quant à elle être défendue grâce à la lutte contre la désinformation. Ici, il propose un renforcement des performances de l'Europe tout entière pour contrer l'intoxication et les manipulations de l'information. Pour clore son propos, le conférencier a tenu à exprimer son indéfectible soutien aux sociétés civiles et aux institutions démocratiques par la promotion des principes démocratiques. Ainsi,

le dernier point, c'est la défense de la démocratie et de l'universalisme. Je le disais, un quart de siècle s'est écoulé et a détruit beaucoup d'illusions. Il y a un quart de siècle, on nous disait que la démocratie était une construction politique qui n'avait vocation qu'à s'étendre, que c'était la fin de l'histoire pour certains, et que tout irait de mieux en mieux. Le réveil a été dur, il n'a pas commencé cette année, mais je ne voudrais pas que nous soyons, à un quart de siècle après, touchés par le syndrome inverse. C'est-à-dire que quand j'entends beaucoup, on n'ose plus quasiment défendre l'État de droit, la démocratie, ce ne serait plus à la mode, et il y a une espèce de fascination mortifère pour l'international des réactionnaires. (E. Macron, p. 20).

Explicitement, Emmanuel Macron pense que la démocratie au XXIe est en berne. Autrefois vu comme le régime adéquat pour le bien-être des populations, la démocratie n'est que l'ombre d'elle-même. Et, les attentes des individus se sont muées en désillusion avec l'absence d'Etat de droit. En effet, il existe une perte de confiance accrue dans les leaders politiques et une crise de la représentation. Cependant, la perte en vitesse du modèle démocratique en Europe ne s'explique-t-il pas également par son impuissance dans la résolution de la guerre en Ukraine.

2 - l'échec de la résolution de la crise ukrainienne

La crise en Ukraine a commencé dès le début de l'année 2014 précisément en février avec l'annexion de la Crimée par la Russie. Ensuite, a suivi le déclenchement d'un conflit à Donbass, dans l'est ukrainien entre les forces de défenses ukrainiennes et des séparatistes pro-russes soutenus par le régime de Poutine. Cette guerre connaît une escalade le 24 février 2022 avec l'invasion de l'armée russe. Elle retient particulièrement l'attention de l'Europe tout entière suivie d'une couverture médiatique importante. Plus clairement,

Le 24 février 2022, ce qui était encore qualifié de tension entre la Russie et le monde occidental à travers l'Ukraine s'est transformé en guerre ouverte avec le déclenchement des premières hostilités sur le territoire ukrainien. Les mises en garde occidentales, les

efforts diplomatiques et les menaces de lourdes sanctions n'ont pas pu empêcher la progression vers l'éclatement d'un conflit.

Ce qui signifie qu'avant la date fatidique du 24 février 2022, la situation politique était crispée entre la Russie et les grandes puissances occidentales en occurrence les États-Unis et l'Union européenne. L'on pouvait alors parler de tensions diplomatiques et politiques, mais la guerre n'avait pas encore été déclarée. Toutefois, la Russie lança le 24 février, une offensive militaire contre l'Ukraine. Ce qui marqua le début d'un conflit ouvert sur le sol ukrainien. Malgré les avertissements des pays occidentaux, les tentatives de négociation et même les menaces de sanction contre la Russie, celle-ci déclencha une guerre que rien a pu arrêter à la fin.

La Russie a montré une résistance en défiant les États-Unis, l'Otan et les pays occidentaux. Elle « *est visiblement restée forte dans la puissance de ses défenses. Nombreux sont tout de même les experts qui estiment que cette situation témoigne aussi de la faiblesse de l'Otan.*» (A. Tognon, 2023). Cela pourrait se justifier du fait que l'Ukraine n'est pas membre de l'Otan, ce qui limite son action quant au soutien indirect (logistique, militaire, renseignement sans envoyer de troupes. Mais plus clairement, l'Otan a évité une confrontation directe avec la Russie par peur d'un élargissement du conflit pouvant aller jusqu'à un conflit mondial et nucléaire.

Dans tous les cas, l'attitude des puissances occidentales traduit une impuissance patente de juguler la montée des États dits révisionnistes qui « *ne jouent plus le jeu politique* » selon les termes du Président Macron et qui piétinent les intérêts des autres pays. Aussi l'expansion du populisme réduit-elle la démocratie.

Le concept de populisme est généralement vu comme une idéologie qui oppose le peuple aux gouvernants. Il prétend que les droits et les libertés individuels et collectifs ne sont pas respectés par les élites sur le plan économique, politique et économique. Cette attitude politique est née :

à la fin du XIXème siècle dans la Russie tsariste et a connu historiquement différentes figures telles que le poujadisme, le péronisme ou le boulangisme. Le populisme entretient un lien étroit avec la démocratie, il représente une tension essentielle de la démocratie : la balance entre la souveraineté populaire et le droit. Le démocrate et le populiste partagent l'idée selon laquelle le peuple est souverain et source de légitimité. (M. Hurard, p.4, 2011).

Il y a environ deux siècles qu'est apparu le populisme dans la Russie avant la révolution de 1917 où le pays était dirigé exclusivement par un empereur détenant le pouvoir absolu. Sous l'appellation de narodnitchestvo, le populisme est un mouvement qui vient du russe narod qui signifiant peuple. Les premiers populistes russes étaient des intellectuels militant contre l'autocratie, c'est-à-dire les régimes politiques dans lesquels les pouvoirs législatif, exécutif et judiciaire sont dirigés par une seule personne. Le populisme entretient un lien étroit avec la démocratie. Son but est de défendre les intérêts du peuple contre les gouvernances corrompues et qui s'éloignent davantage des réalités socio-politiques du peuple.

Durant ces deux dernières décennies, la démocratie est secouée par le populisme qui ne cesse de s'étendre. Elle connaît en réalité un déclin non seulement en Europe où elle a été conçue mais également, dans le reste du monde. En Allemagne, le parti Alternative für Deutschland (AFD), parti nationaliste fondé en 2013, est devenu est en 2025 le deuxième parti le plus important du pays. En Belgique, Bart De Wever leader du parti nationaliste est devenu en février 2025, premier ministre. En Roumanie, le candidat populiste George Simion, leader de l'Alliance pour l'unité des Roumains, est actuellement en lice pour la présidence de la Republique. En Hongrie et en Pologne, le premier ministre Victor Orbán au pouvoir depuis 2010 et Jaroslaw Kaczyński du parti Droit et Justice (PIS), exercent incarnent les valeurs du nationalisme. On dénombre aussi de nombreux cas de figures tels que Donald Trump aux Etats-Unis, Giorgia Meloni en Italie, Jair Bolsonaro au Brésil, Mark Carney au Canada, Narendra Modi en Inde et Javier Milei en Argentine.

Vu ce qui précède, la démocratie en Europe et dans le reste du monde tend aujourd'hui à se réduire et même à disparaître. Le discours du Président français Emmanuel Macron en fait l'état actuel avec plus de désolation que d'espoir. Et, l'une des raisons fondamentales reste l'expansion du populisme dirigé par le Président Donald Trump, viril défenseur des causes et des intérêts proprement américains. Cependant, la rupture du spectre de la démocratie constitue un réel atout pour certains Etats africains qui progressivement se délient de l'impérialisme pour aborder avec espoir le chemin de l'émancipation.

III - L'Afrique en Renaissance : entre émancipation et nouveaux défis

L'histoire de l'Afrique est celle d'une marche escarpée qui depuis les premiers pas du colonialisme jusqu'à l'ère actuel, ne manque de sombres tâches et d'éclats de joie. Plus de soixante dix ans après les indépendances, l'expérience laisse voir que l'émancipation des sociétés africaines n'a été qu'un vague concept dénué de réalité formelle. Toutefois, depuis le premier mandat du Président Donald Trump et les bouleversements ayant surgi dans le monde, certains pays africains tentent malgré les énormes défis endogènes et exogènes de s'inscrire dans le chemin de la liberté. Cela offre des perspectives de réécriture de l'histoire africaine, un continent qui à l'ère de la technologie numérique, ne pense plus choir sur le faix de la souffrance.

1 - Les crises mondiales et la réorganisation du continent

La crise que connaît la démocratie partout dans le monde entraîne un désengagement progressif des anciennes puissances coloniales et une affiliation à de nouveaux partenaires. En effet, certains pays africains tels que l'Algérie, le Tchad, Éthiopie, la Guinée Conakry et la République centrafricaine affirment au quotidien une ferme volonté de s'affranchir généralement de l'influence américaine et française. Malgré ce ballonnement du peuple africain par des brimades impérialistes, certains dirigeants tâtonnent pour guider leurs populations. Ils se trouvent malgré tous les risques afférents, d'autres horizons pour tisser des partenariats susceptibles de créer les conditions de développement. Depuis 2009 par exemple, la Chine est devenue le premier partenaire commercial de l'Afrique. La Russie développe un partenariat militaire, économique et diplomatiques dans des pays tels que la Centrafrique. Le Mali, le Burkina Faso et le Niger ont rompu les accords militaires avec la France pour la Chine, la Russie et la Turquie. L'Afrique du Sud et Éthiopie ont fait leur entrée dans les Brics, groupe de puissances émergentes visant à rééquilibrer l'ordre mondial dominé par les géants européens et créant un développement économique équitable entre les membres.

Cette recherche de nouveaux partenaires en défiant les anciennes puissances coloniales montrent que la démocratie telle qu'élaborée en Afrique n'est qu'illusion. Elle n'a jamais formellement existé. Ce fait s'explique du fait de l'assassinat des nombreuses élites dans le but de juguler toute velléité d'émancipation des africains. Et, pour la marche vers la liberté, plus de vingt Présidents africains ont été éliminés brutalement pour n'avoir pas parfois coopéré avec le colon. Sylvanus Olympio au Togo en 1963, Johnson Aguiyi-Ironsi au Nigéria en 1966, Abdirashid AliShermarke en Somalie en 1969, Abeid AMmani Karume au Zanzibar en 1972, Richard Ratsimandrava au Madagascar en 1975, François Tombalbaye au Tchad en 1975, Murtala Mohammed au Nigéria en 1976, Marien Ngouabi au Congo -Brazzaville en 1977, Teferi Banti en Ethiopie en 1977, Anouar el Sadate en Egypte en 1981, Thomas Sankara au Burkina Faso en 1987, Ahmed Abdallah au Comores en 1989, Samuel Doe au Libéria en 1990, Mohamed Boudiaf en Algérie en 1992, Melchior Ndadaye au Burundi en 1993, Juvénal Habyarimana au Rwanda en 1994, Cyprien Ntaryamira au Burundi en 1994, Ibrahim Baré Maïnassara au Niger en 1999, Laurent Désiré Kabila au Congo-Kinshassa en 2001, João Bernardo Viera en Guinée Bissau en 2009 et enfin Mouammar Kadhafi en

Libye en 2011. À côté de ce triste chapitre, l'on dénombre des leaders d'opinions tels que Lumumba, Biaka Bida et autres assassinés pour avoir défendus les valeurs et les intérêts de leur société.

Aujourd'hui, l'alliance des États du Sahel (AES) est une organisation inter-étatique créée le 16 septembre 2023 par le Burkina Faso, le Mali et le Niger. Sortie du bras de la Communauté économique des États de l'Afrique de l'Ouest (CEDEAO) . Après le coup d'Etat du 26 juillet 2023 ayant renversé le Président Mohamed Bazoum par le général Abdourahamane Tchiani, certains États tels que la Côte d'Ivoire et la France ont menacé de rétablir l'ordre constitutionnel. Ainsi, le Burkina Faso et le Mali ont manifesté leur volonté de soutenir le général nigérien dans sa visée d'assurer la sécurité de son territoire. Cet acte a conduit finalement à la création d'une fédération dans l'objectif d'« *établir une architecture de défense collective et d'assistance mutuelle aux Parties contractantes* ». (Capitaine I. Traoré et al, p. 3). En substance, l'AES est une confédération qui vise à protéger son territoire, défendre ses intérêts et s'affirmer comme un pays digne et libre sur le plan politique, économique et social. Elle constitue pour les générations futures une voie.x indéniable de liberté avec les perspectives de libération qu'elle ouvre aujourd'hui.

2 - Perspectives pour une Afrique libérée

La sphère politique africaine suffoque des coups d'Etat militaires et civils. De la naissance des pays africains à l'état actuel, l'on dénombre en Afrique plus de 220 tentatives de coups d'Etat dont 109 réussi et 111 échoués selon les chercheurs américains Jonathan Powell et Clayton Thyne. Cela traduit une atmosphère hostile à l'épanouissement des populations. Même si ces perturbations sont parfois causées par des africains eux-mêmes dans leurs quêtes démesurée du pouvoir, celles sont dans bien des cas orchestrées et justifiées par la métropole dans le but de maintenir le pays secoué dans la dépendance. Ainsi, la reconstitution du climat africain passe par la limitation des mandats présidentiels. Aujourd'hui certains pays connaissent des présidents avec plus de trois mandats exprimant la ferme volonté à maintenir leur pays dans une sorte de monarchie entraînant même des guerres civiles, des enlèvements, des emprisonnements arbitraires, des assassinats. En Côte d'Ivoire le Président Alassane Ouattara au pouvoir depuis 2011, Paul Biya au Cameroun depuis 1982, Paul Kagamé au Rwanda depuis 2000 et en Guinée équatoriale avec Teodoro Obiang Nguema Mbasogo depuis 1979. Est-ce à dire que le manque d'alternance politique dans ces pays indique l'absence de candidats potentiels à diriger efficacement le pouvoir ? Evidemment non.

De nombreux États africains croupissent dans un endettement économique sans précédent du fait de leur incapacité à créer pour le bien-être de leurs populations, des conditions optimales. L'on évoque également le manque de volonté politique et nationaliste. En Côte d'Ivoire, des Présidents tels qu'Henri Konan Bédié ont remboursé toutes les dettes extérieures; et cela s'est fait suivant le nationalisme politico-économique promu de 1993 à 1999. C'est bel et bien le chemin ce modèle de développement qu'empruntent les élites soucieuses du destin de leur peuple.

Pour sortir du cycle de l'endettement massif, les États africains doivent mener des réformes structurelles et stratégiques adaptées aux besoins des populations. Pour ce faire, il revient d'abord de réformer la gouvernance économique : lutter contre la corruption et les détournements de fonds, limiter les dépenses des ministères, diversifier l'économie par la réduction de la dépendance aux matières premières, développer l'agriculture, l'industrie locale, soutenir les petites et moyennes entreprises et enfin protéger les droits des investisseurs tout en veillant à l'intérêt national. Pour la Fondation pour le Renforcement des Capacités en Afrique, « *Certains pays africains ont des états développementalistes forts qui organisent les activités économiques et régulent le secteur privé et d'autres acteurs du développement comme les organisateurs de la société civile* ». Autrement dit, l'Etat doit organiser le secteur économique en encourageant et protégeant les petites entreprises contre les grandes multinationales. Il doit réguler les secteurs publics et privés pour donner la chance à tout le monde de bénéficier des mêmes avantages du marché.

Par ailleurs, l'un des éléments fondamentaux sur lesquels repose le développement réside dans l'éducation. Celle-ci constitue un levier important de liberté. L'éducation libère l'esprit des chaînes de l'ignorance, de la dépendance et la manipulation à telle enseigne qu'un peuple éduqué ou instruit est capable de faire un choix éclairé dans des élections et de participer librement à l'édification de la vie de sa nation. L'éducation occupe une place de choix dans la prise de décision des africains puisqu'elle permet de découvrir son passé, comprendre les réalités socio-politiques et économiques présentes et s'orienter quant à la construction de son avenir. Elle est le moteur de la transformation sociale par le facteur de l'égalité des chances dans l'insertion dans le tissu social. En Afrique, les grandes masses manipulées pendant les périodes d'élection présidentielles sont victimes du manque d'instruction.

Enfin, le retour aux cultures endogènes constitue un argument de poids pour l'indépendance réelle de l'Afrique. Celle-ci soit s'appuyer inévitablement sur ses propres cultures. Ce qui est réjouissant de nos jours, ce sont la majorité des colloques dans l'univers scientifique et académique qui font la promotion des cultures endogènes. Cela constitue une porte d'ouverture à l'implantation des valeurs citoyennes aux populations africaines.

Conclusion

Depuis environ une décennie, l'arène politique mondiale a été secouée par l'arrivée du 45e Président américain Donald Trump. Nationaliste avec son modèle de gouvernance « America First ». Ce protectionnisme économique s'explique par sa priorité de réviser les bases du multilatéralisme en remettant en cause toutes les règles de coopération avec les grandes puissances telles que la Chine et l'Europe. Aussi s'ajoute le souverainisme géopolitique fondé sur la déstabilisation des alliances traditionnelles envers l'OTAN et le retrait de l'accord de Paris sur le climat et l'annonce de la fin de l'accord nucléaire avec l'Iran. Il développe une politique migratoire protectionniste par la construction et le renforcement du mur à la frontière mexicaine et la politique de séparation de familles clandestins. Ainsi,

lorsque le républicain Donald Trump prend ses fonctions de président des États-Unis en janvier 2017, ses discours de campagne précédents laissent entendre qu'il allait pratique une forme d'isolationnisme, en retirant le pays de plusieurs institutions multilatérales, aussi bien internationales que régionales, ainsi que de certains accords internationaux. Son souhait est de marquer le repli des États-Unis des affaires extérieures, et de

redonner la priorité aux Américains. (R. Perron, 2018).
En clair, Donald trump, lors de ces deux gouvernances reste fidèle à sa politique nationaliste. Cette vision s'inscrit dans la continuité de la science médicale de Claude Bernard. À caractère endogène, la médecine expérimentale repose sur les phénomènes vitaux, régis par des règles internes à l'organisme. Indépendant des conditions climatiques externes, le milieu intérieur est un environnement stable qui assure son bon fonctionnement et son équilibre par son système qui lui est propre. Par ce fait, la maladie et la santé trouve leur origine dans les phénomènes physiologiques. la science médicale bernardienne est marquée par la physiologie expérimentale. En un mot, la physiologie expérimentale telle que développée par Claude Bernard, constitue la base analytique de la médecine scientifique. En effet, la physiologie permet de comprendre la structure et le fonctionnement organique à l'état normal. Cet éclairage physiologique guide à la connaissance des mécanismes pathologiques ainsi que les mécanismes thérapeutiques. Dans la physiologie, « *la fixité du milieu intérieur est la condition de la vie libre, indépendante* ». (C. Bernard, 1966, p. 113). Autrement dit, le milieu intérieur est régi par une fixité qui rend l'organisme libre.
La politique trumpiste a accentué le déclin de la démocratie en Europe. Le discours du Président français

Emmanuel Macron lors de la 30ᵉ conférence des ambassadrices et des ambassadeurs, fait état du bouleversement des puissances européennes. En effet, l'ordre international fondé sur des règles est remis en cause. L'incapacité de l'Europe dans la résolution de la crise ukrainienne est un thème récurrent dans les analyses géopolitiques depuis 2022 puisqu'elle dépend stratégiquement des États-Unis. Les pays européens depuis le conflit Russie-Ukraine, se sont alignés sur la politique américaine. C'est pourquoi Emmanuel Macron recommande la nécessité pour l'Europe de sortir de sa naïveté et de s'affirmer comme puissance autonome.

Depuis 2011, les présidents américains successifs nous disent tous la même chose. Leur priorité est d'abord les États-Unis d'Amérique, puis la relation avec la chine. L'Europe a un autre rang, une autre place. Soyons suffisamment lucides pour le voir et donc œuvrons en étant cohérents. (E. Macron, 2025, p.4)

Selon les mots du Président Emmanuel Macron, la politique des présidents américains qui se sont succédé ont vu comme primauté, ses propres intérêts et cela passe par les relations bilatérales avec la Chine, partenaire sérieux pour son poids économique mondial et pour son influence géopolitique croissante. Enfin, la rupture démocratique qui crée un monde « *un monde en désordre* » selon l'expression d'Emmanuel Macron, est une opportunité pour certains pays africains. Ceux-ci tentent de construire leur destin en se défiant des anciennes puissances coloniales pour de nouveaux partenariats. C'est le cas du Mali, du Burkina Faso et du Niger qui sont les principaux dissidents. Leurs affiliations aux nouvelles puissances émergentes dénotent la tentative désespérée d'une réelle liberté quand l'on sait que l'Afrique gît sous le coup d'une violence inouïe administrée aux panafricanistes depuis l'aube des indépendances jusqu'à l'ère actuelle.

Pour notre part, la philosophie politique de Donald Trump cernée à la lumière de la médecine expérimentale de Claude Bernard apparaît comme un modèle crédible pour la gestion des sociétés actuelles résolument tournées vers la technologie. Bien évidemment, la mondialisation reste une priorité, mais une nation pour se bâtir a nécessairement besoin d'abord d'un fondement endogène.

Bibliographie

BERNARD Claude, *Introduction à l'étude de la médecine expérimentale,* Chronologie et préface par François Dagognet, Paris, Garnier Flammarion, 1984.

BERNARD Claude, *Leçons sur les phénomènes de la vie communs aux animaux et aux végétaux*, Avec une préface de Georges Canguilhem, 1966, p. 113.

BERNARD Claude, *Principes de médecine expérimentale*, Paris, PUF, 1947.

Capitaine TRAORÉ Ibrahim, Colonel GOITA Assimi, Général TIANI Abdourahamane, Charte du Liptako-Gourma instituant l'alliance des Etats du sahel entre : le Burkina Faso, la République du Mali, La République du Niger in https://www.rtb.bf/wp-content/uploads/2023/09/Charte-de-création-de-lalliance-des-Etat-du-sahel.pdf.

Fondation pour le renforcement des capacités en Afrique, 2017, *les moteurs de la croissance économique en Afrique : opportunités, financement et capacités*, Harare. En ligne : https://www.theacbf.org

HURARE Marine, 2011, *La montée des populismes en Europe*. En ligne : https : www.pourlasolidarité.eu/wpcontent/uploads/2015/05/09_2011_AffairesSociales_MonteeDesPopulismesEnEuro pe.

JANSEN Sabine, 2019, *Les États-Unis de Donald Trump : America First et hégémonie décomplexée*. In https//:www.vie-publique.fr/paroledexpert/269992-les États-Unis de Donald Trump : America First et hégémonie décomplexée | vie-publique.fr

N'GBO Aké Gilbert, lors du colloque international organisé par l'ASCAD (Académie des Sciences, des Arts, des Cultures d'Afrique et des Diasporas africaines portant sur la thématique : Cultures endogènes et éducation en Afrique, du 27 au 29 novembre 2024 à l'université Félix Houphouet Boigny.

PERRON Régine, 2018, *La fin du multilatéralisme : une victoire de Donald Trump ? 2018* .En ligne: https://www.euromed-ihedn.fr/files/18-11-04---Diploweb--fin-multilateralisme-victoire-de-Trump-.pdf

SMITH R. Bryan, 2020, *Le bilan économique du premier mandat de Trump*. En ligne : https://the conversation.com/le-bilan-economique-du-premier-mandat-de-trump-147635.

TARDIS Matthieu, 2020, *La politique américaine d'immigration : la fabrique d'une crise,* Notes de l'Ifri, Ifri.

TOGNON Armel, 2023, *Ukraine : échec de l'Otan face à la Russie ou échec de la contre-offensive de Kiev ?* En ligne: https://lanouvelletribune.info.

WRIGHT Thomas cité par Martin Quencez, Le «trumpisme» en politique étrangère:vision et pratiqueFrance Ouest, https://www.ouest-france.fr/monde/etats-unis/donald-trump-reorganise-sa-strategie-militaire-et-souhaite-delaisser-leurope-au-profit-de-la-chine-1891cf4c-0fd

www.eiforce.gov.cm/wp-content/uploads/2022/03Note-danalyse-Guerre-Russie-Ukraine-Dr-Fofack-Eric-Wilson-pour-Eiforces.pdf

Docteur Luc KOFFI est originaire du centre de la Côte d'Ivoire. Enseignant-Chercheur au département de philosophie à l'Université Péléforo Gon Coulibaly, il est membre du Laboratoire de Logiques, Savoirs, Rationalités (L.S.R), Université Alassane Ouattara (Bouaké-Côte d'Ivoire). Il est également membre de l'Association des Écrivains de Côte d'Ivoire depuis 2019. Il est l'auteur du Roman *L'Univers des Mouches*, Bouaké, Éditions Papyrus, 2019.

Mmap Multi-disciplinary Series

If you have enjoyed *Donald Trump's Second Coming, Is Democracy Dead, Dying or Alive,* consider these other fine books in the **Mmap Multi-disciplinary Series** from *Mwanaka Media and Publishing:*

Africanization and Americanization Anthology Volume 1, Searching for Interracial, Interstitial, Intersectional and Interstates Meeting Spaces, Africa Vs North America by Tendai R Mwanaka
A Conversation..., A Contact by Tendai Rinos Mwanaka
Africa, UK and Ireland: Writing Politics and Knowledge Production Vol 1 by Tendai R Mwanaka
Writing Language, Culture and Development, Africa Vs Asia Vol 1 by Tendai R Mwanaka, Wanjohi wa Makokha and Upal Deb
Zimbolicious: An Anthology of Zimbabwean Literature and Arts, Vol 3 by Tendai Mwanaka
Drawing Without Licence by Tendai R Mwanaka
Writing Grandmothers/ Escribiendo sobre nuestras raíces: Africa Vs Latin America Vol 2 by Tendai R Mwanaka and Felix Rodriguez
Tiny Human Protection Agency by Megan Landman
Ghetto Symphony by Mandla Mavolwane
A Portrait of Defiance by Tendai Rinos Mwanaka

Nationalism: (Mis)Understanding Donald Trump's Capitalism, Racism, Global Politics, International Trade and Media Wars, Africa Vs North America Vol 2 by Tendai R Mwanaka
Ouafa and Thawra: About a Lover From Tunisia by Arturo Desimone
Zimbolicious: An Anthology of Zimbabwean Literature and Arts, Vol 4 by Tendai Mwanaka and Jabulani Mzinyathi
Chitungwiza Mushamukuru Anthology by Tendai Rinos Mwanaka
The Day and the Dweller: A Study of the Emerald Tablets by Jonathan Thompson
Zimbolicious: An Anthology of Zimbabwean Literature and Arts, Vol 5 by Tendai Mwanaka
Robotics Anthology, Africa vs Asia Vol 2 by Tendai Rinos Mwanaka
Shaping Up by Tendai Rinos Mwanaka
Zimbolicious Anthology Vol 6: An Anthology of Zimbabwean Literature and Arts by Tendai Rinos Mwanaka and Chenjerai Mhondera
Registers of Loss: PhotoTalking to the Baobab Trees of Nyatate by Tendai Rinos Mwanaka
The Trick is to Keep Breathing: Covid 19 Stories From African and North American Writers, vol 3 by Tendai Rinos Mwanaka

Fixing Earth: An Anthology of Ireland, UK and Africa Writers, Vol 2 by Tendai Rinos Mwanaka

Zimbolicious: An Anthology of Zimbabwean Literature and Arts, Vol 7 Tendai Rinos Mwanaka and Tanaka Chidora

Writing Woman Anthology: Personal Essays and Short stories, An Anthology of African and Asian Writers, Vol 3 by Tendai Rinos Mwanaka, Abigail George, Sue Zhu and Monalisa Jena

Writing Woman Anthology: Drama and Scholarly Essays, An Anthology of African and Asian Writers, Vol 3 by Tendai Rinos Mwanaka, Abigail George, Sue Zhu and Monalisa Jena

WRITING WOMAN ANTHOLOGY: Poetry and Visual art by Tendai Rinos Mwanaka, Abigail George, Sue Zhu and Monalisa Jena

Zimbolicious: An Anthology of Zimbabwean Literature and Arts, Vol 8 by Tendai Rinos Mwanaka and Matthew Kunashe Chikono

Of poets, gods, ghosts. Irritants and storytellers by Tendai Rinos Mwanaka

The Aporia of Unnamed Things by Tendai Rinos Mwanaka

Glyphs of Love by Tendai Rinos Mwanaka

Zimbolicious Anthology Vol 9 by Tendai Rinos Mwanaka

Men: An Anthology of African and Latin American writers vol 3 by Tendai Rinos Mwanaka and Ingrid Bringas

Upcoming

https://facebook.com/MwanakaMediaAndPublishing/

www.ingramcontent.com/pod-product-compliance
Lightning Source LLC
Chambersburg PA
CBHW052049220426
43663CB00012B/2501